ACHIEVING SUCCESS THROUGH ADVERSITY

KENNETH R. SHELTON, SR.

Foreword by Les Brown

www.kensrspeaks.com

2009

Achieving Success Through Adversity
By Kenneth R. Shelton, Sr.

Copyright © 2009 by Kenneth R. Shelton, Sr. & K. R. Shelton International

All Rights Reserved
No parts of this book may be reproduced or utilized in any form or by any means, electronic or mechanical, including photocopying and recording, or by any information storage and retrieval system without permission in writing from the publisher.

Inquiries should be addressed to:
K. R. Shelton International
P. O. Box 533
Muskegon, Michigan 49443
Ph. 313.427.1671
www.kensrspeaks.com

www.achievingsuccessthroughadversity.com

Manufactured in the United States of America
This book is printed on acid free paper

Library of Congress Cataloging in Publication Data
10 9 8 7 6 5 4 3 2 1
ISBN: 978-0-615-30543-1

Dedication

*To my mother, Ida B. Shelton,
and my late father, Jessie Shelton.*

*Momma, I want to thank you for the love you have
shown me and the demonstration of a true believer.*

*Daddy, I want to thank you for showing me
how to be a man.*

Contents

Acknowledgements VII
Foreword by Les Brown IX
Introduction XI

Chapter One
   Twists and Turns in the Road of Life 1

Chapter Two
   We Need to Be True to Ourselves 15

Chapter Three
   Do Not Play the Blame Game 29

Chapter Four
   Do You Really Want Success? 41

Chapter Five
   The Power from Within 55

Chapter Six
   Using Our Time Wisely 69

CHAPTER SEVEN
   WISDOM 79

CHAPTER EIGHT
   ENJOY THE JOURNEY 91

CHAPTER NINE
   KEYS TO SUCCESS 103

CHAPTER TEN
   YOU MUST HAVE THE RIGHT PICTURE 113

AUTHOR BIOGRAPHY 123

SELECTED QUOTATIONS 125

ACKNOWLEDGEMENTS

I want to thank:

Mr. Les Brown for being a remarkable mentor, friend and someone who has encouraged me to lighten-up.

Ms. Jeanette Riley for editorial assistance and loyal friendship.

Ms. Connie Jones for many hours of work to perfect this project.

My sister Joyce Hunter for her calming voice during difficult times.

My Pastor & Mrs. Charles Poole and the Bethesda Baptist Church for your love and support.

To Bishop Nathaniel W. Wells Jr., a great mentor and friend.

ACKNOWLEDGEMENTS

To Mr. James Branch Rowan for being a reader.

To Dwight Pledger for being a true brother.

To Rene Godefroy for his assistance and tremendous insight.

To my cousins, Robert Earl Pompey for being a big brother, and Otis Pompey for toughening me up (I grew up in a home without a brother).

Murone Ali, thank you for giving me "The Autobiography of Malcolm X" that inspired my desire to read.

My Aunt Ella for always supporting me.

Commissioner Bill Gill for helping during one of the most difficult times in my life.

Bishop Willie Burrel for being a true man of faith.

Mrs. Jean Johnson for words of encouragement

Allan De Giulio, Ph. D. for countless hours of proofreading and editing.

I would also like to extend a heart felt thank you to the many people of Muskegon, Michigan who have helped make me the man that I became.

Foreword

It has been said that "adversity introduces a man to himself." If ever there was a man made by adversity it is, Ken Shelton, Sr. I have met many people and heard many stories as I have traveled across this nation and around the world. When Ken shared the story of how he was able to overcome a series of setbacks that would have destroyed the average person, it reminded me of what my friend Willie Jolley meant when he said, "A setback is a setup for a comeback."

Ken's overcoming his challenges was only half the battle, but his achieving success through adversity is what sets him apart from many who have not learned the magic of embracing challenges. I know firsthand what it means to be hit with setback after setback. When I had my television talk show cancelled, when I was diagnosed with prostate cancer, when I lost my beloved mother Mamie Brown to breast cancer, I had to turn my pain into power, and see these obstacles as challenges to embrace and ultimately overcome.

You will gain priceless insights from Ken as he walks you through his own personal journey and shares lessons learned from years of study and application of the power principles that

Foreword

have brought him and others success. He teaches you to look at life's challenges with new eyes and a greater sense of confidence so that you will not only overcome them, but use them to launch you into greatness.

Achieving Success Through Adversity may be the single most important resource you will need to accomplish and live your dreams. As a mentor and friend of Ken Shelton I have personally benefited from his extensive collection of books, CDs, DVDs, and his wide variety of personal development tools. I teach people to "live full and die empty." Ken Shelton, Sr., has taken that instruction to heart by pouring himself into this work. You will literally be transformed chapter by chapter, and never again look at life's challenges in the same way.

Achieving Success Through Adversity will help you to develop a positive mind set and give you the power to live your dreams. We need more men and women like Ken who will do all they can with what they have from where they are. I want Ken to know that he has not only done me proud but has also taken his place among the giants in the personal development industry who have through their many sacrifices left their mark in the minds of the masses.

This is Ms. Mamie Brown's baby boy saying to Ken Shelton, Sr., "God bless you and God bless the day you were born."

LES BROWN

Introduction

I want to thank you for taking the time to read this book. It is my hope that it will assist you in navigating through some of the difficulties of life. First, you must have the right thinking process. It is important not to allow our spirits to be broken if we are to make it through tough times. I have had my ups and downs in life and I realize that some people make irreversible decisions that they may regret for a lifetime. I remember an old song that includes the phrase "you can be flying high in April and be shot down in May." This journey called life has peaks and valleys. Some of the unfortunate circumstances of life can turn out to be a blessing if we do not become frustrated and give up.

This book is written after 30 years of researching why some succeed and others fail. I have tried to explain the process "Achieving Success Through Adversity" in simple terms. In all my studies I have not come across anyone who achieved greatness without overcoming adversity. Sadly, I have also observed some who have achieved greatness at one point in life and later fall into a pit of despair. This happened because their thinking became defective. Earl Nightingale, one of the giants in the human development movement, is the author of "The Strangest Secret," the first spoken audio to sell a million

Introduction

copies and receive a gold record. In that audio, Mr. Nightingale states that we become what we think about. Whatever dominant thought you have in your mind will determine your destiny. It is so important not to perceive a temporary situation as permanent. It is like taking a picture and saying that it can tell what the future holds. The only thing the picture can tell is what is happening at that moment.

Do not give up on life because of what is happening in the moment, for what seems like a curse today can turn out to be a blessing tomorrow.

KENNETH R. SHELTON, SR.

Chapter One

Twists and Turns in the Road of Life

"No matter how things seem to be or actually are raise your sights and see the possibilities, always see for they're always there."

Norman Vincent Peale

TWISTS AND TURNS IN THE ROAD OF LIFE

Often we want to live a life that goes from birth straight to success. We want to take the easy, scenic route. I have lived long enough to know that there are twist and turns, and lumps and bumps along the road of life. New circumstances will come into your life, and those circumstances will reveal if you truly have a solid foundation.

About 27 years ago, I remember sitting in my home all alone crying because it seemed no one understood. I had become delusional and had lost sight of reality. I started believing that someone was trying to kill me. It was my own imagination. I was hearing voices even though I was home alone. It was as if I had a kind of telepathic power and could hear voices and messages without a telephone. I remember looking at the ceiling of my home and messages were coming through the walls and entering my mind. Depression is a terrible illness, and many lives are destroyed by not handling the disappointments in life correctly.

We need to be careful about the "what ifs" of life. What if this happens? What if that happens? Many are destroyed by the "what ifs" Many things that people worry about never happen. It is just needless worry. I once owned a white handled 38 caliber pistol. I lent the gun to my cousin who pawned it and said the shop owner would not sell it back. I was very upset, but that loss turned out to be a blessing. When I lost my mind, I am sure I would have killed someone if I still had that gun. I was home alone when a neighbor came to visit. I believed that neighbor was a part of some great conspiracy against me. I feel strongly that I might have shot that neighbor if I had that gun.

As stated previously, I was very delusional. I had the impression that a force field surrounded me and I would not die even if someone shot me. I understand how people can do things that are very crazy. I loaded my car thinking I had to get out of Muskegon because of the conspiracy to kill me. I started driving to Youngstown, Ohio, where I thought I would be safe. Along the way to Ohio, I got out of my car at the side of the road and cried. The tears were many and fell like Niagara Falls. I was seriously thinking someone was trying to kill me.

People try to analyze tears but tears are the agony that has built up in the body and escapes through our eyes. I was blessed that no police officer saw me. Surely they would have taken me to a mental institution. I got back in my car and finished my drive to Ohio. I thought I would find help there, but I did not. I have found the only place where you can always find help is through the Higher Power...God! How many people have been crushed because they believed they could go to someone and find help but instead they found disappointment?

In Ohio, I found no help there, so I spent the night at my uncle's home, and the next day I drove back to Muskegon. My behavior became so bizarre that I found myself in a mental facility. There I was diagnosed as paranoid schizophrenic. I felt humiliated because I was a preacher who taught people to trust in God during difficult times, and during my test I earned an 'F' for failure. I had a nervous breakdown. I told others to trust in God, and then it was revealed that I obviously didn't trust in Jehovah myself. It is true as it says in Philippians 4:13 that "I can do all things through Christ which strengthens me." However, you must really believe.

You might be curious how I found myself in this kind of situation. It was a blessing, but I am sure most would ask the question, "Is he still crazy to say it was a blessing." I truly believe Roman 8:28, which states, "All things work together for good to them that love God, to them who are called according to his purpose." I say it was a blessing because it caused me to change my whole perspective about responding to the stresses of life. Now, I let very few things stress me. I evaluate the situation. Can I change it, and if so, what must I do? If I cannot change the situation, then I adjust and accept it. People get upset about what other people do and because they have no control over them. Not me. If I give a loved one or friend advice and he or she decides not to take it, I am not going to lose any sleep because it is his or her choice. Life is determined by the choices we make, whether good or bad.

I know a truth is a truth whether a person believes it or not. A few years ago during a storm, a red flag was raised indicating people should not swim in the water of one of our lakes. One young man chose to disregard the flag. Unfortunately, he drowned. Many times in life we can see warning signs and we ignore them. Although the young man did not believe (heed)

the warning sign that it was a dangerous situation, it did not stop it from being true. Sometimes in life it seems as if we are in stormy seas and in desperate need of a life jacket. Many end up drowning even though life jackets were available to them. The "life jackets" are there, but some do not put them on.

There are ways to cope with life's problems that are similar to using a life jacket. If we do not use them, the problems of this world can cause us to "drown" in a sea of misery. We must protect our minds and hearts from being overwhelmed by the problems of this world. We must take care of our minds and be careful what we spend our time thinking about. Do you know if you destroy cells in the brain, they will not grow back? We can cut our hair or nails, and they will grow back, but brain cells are different. Many people who have gone through what I experienced are not able to talk about it. Some never come back to their right mind, and others may have heart attacks, strokes, or die.

I am able to say that many people are not as blessed as I am. If we do not handle the stresses of life properly, they will overwhelm us. Pretending stress does not exist or ignoring it, will not make the stress go away. I find so many people are in denial. It is like an ostrich who sees danger coming and sticks its head in the sand hoping the problem will go away. Stress is destructive to our bodies and causes illnesses, such as hardening of the arteries and so many other ailments. I read that people go to the doctor's office seventy percent of the time because of stress. Stress can also be the reason some people find comfort in eating or in substance abuse. Years ago, when I first accepted my call to the ministry, I was under the impression that every preacher was just like God. I did not truly take notice of the scripture that says, "Some are wolves in sheep clothing."

During that time, my father was dying of liver disease from drinking alcohol. A year before my father died, I told him that if he kept drinking, he would be dead within a year. When you are young, you always want to be right, but when you get older, you wish sometimes you were wrong. Within the year, I was in the hospital looking at my father who had all kinds of tubes inserted in his nose. I have often said if a person watched someone die of cirrhosis of the liver, he or she would never drink.

Many people think that alcohol and drugs will give them an answer to their problems, but they only offer death and destruction. They believe they can make it through adversity and experience greatness by drinking or doing drugs, but it will not happen. My father thought Seagram's gin would help him through his problems. I remember talking to him in the hospital, and he said because of his sixth grade education he had not understood what I was saying to him about the destructiveness of alcohol. At the end of his life my father realized too late that you cannot overcome adversity and experience greatness by ingesting a foreign substance.

Sometimes people try drugs to get them through their adversity. Sometimes people turn to a certain person. My source and strength comes from my relationship with God. Many refer to it as a <u>Higher Power</u>. I thank God that I have a mother that believes in God because many times when I was young and it was difficult, she would say you need to talk to God to help you solve your problems.

If we are going to make it through adversity, we often have to change our pattern of thinking. It is unrealistic to believe that we can keep doing things in the same way and get a different result. So often people are afraid to change. Many times people stay in relationships because they are afraid to change, and they believe the only way to get through their adversity is by staying in the relationship even though in their hearts they know it is not good for them. No one can live life without disappointment and heartache. The way you will get through will depend on your mental approach. If you are going to make it through your adversity, you need to realize there is no one person who is always going to be available to assist you.

I worked extremely hard to get an agency started, including securing funding for the agency. I was promised that if I was successful in this effort, I would receive the job of Executive Director with a certain starting salary. Once the agency funding was secured, those in power reneged and offered me the position at half the salary originally promised. I was crushed because I had recently accepted my call to the ministry and because I was dealing with pastors. I felt there was no need to take extra precautions because these were men of God, and certainly, they would not double-cross me.

I have learned that just because a person calls himself something it does not always make it so. I could sit in a chicken coop forever, and it still would not make me a chicken. Needless to say, I decided not to take the job. This resulted in my having so much hate that it almost destroyed me. I call this the "young and dumb" period of my life. I suffered for a number of years because of that decision. Perhaps I should have taken the job until I could find something better.

I had to learn that everything that is good for me, I might not necessarily enjoy. For example, you might not enjoy going to the doctor and getting a shot, but it could be good for you. After much crying and hurt, it turned out to be a good thing because I learned there are some things you must give to God to handle when you have done everything you can do. A merry heart is good for the soul. This is not just lip service. We should actually give the problem to God after we have done our part! My nervous breakdown reminded me that I am not superhuman.

The real test in life is whether we can overcome the major setbacks in life that are bound to occur. We must never forget God has a plan for our life. Even disappointments have a part in our life in fulfilling our destiny. We know that sand must get into the oyster shell to make a pearl. It takes pressure on coal to make a diamond. So too, pressure can either make us or break us. I remember Pastor J. C. Wade's statement that a test will either prove us or improve us.

The mistake many people make when they are in a crisis is they believe the crisis will last forever. It is darkest before the dawn of day. In Viktor Frankl's book, "Man's Search for Meaning," he writes about abuse in the concentration camps. Many people got frostbite and had their limbs cut off. Dr. Frankl developed what he called the logos theory, which proposed that there is going to be a better day. No matter what kind of situation we find ourselves in, we must believe there is going to be a better day. We should live by revelation rather than by our situation. The situation may not be the what we want, but we understand that when God gets ready to elevate us no one can stop Him.

We cannot let our spirit be broken because if our spirit is broken, we will give up on life. Achieving success through adversity is not always easy. In Orison Swett Marden's book,

How To Get Whatever You Want, he says, "We demagnetize ourselves by wrong thinking and lack of faith. We are the only obstacles in our path and we forget that the person working with God is greater than any obstacle that can oppose itself to his will."

We must never forget that our thoughts produce our reality. What we visualize constantly becomes our reality. We attract whatever is our dominant thought. If we are going to make it through adversity, we must keep moving. One of my favorite scriptures is Romans 4:18: "Who against hope believed in hope, that he might become the father of many nations, according to that which was spoken, So shall thy seed be." What the scripture is saying is that no matter how dark it is, we must continue to believe a better day is coming. Once we lose hope, it is all over. Regardless of the situation, you must hold on to your faith. However, we must be willing to change.

I remember one day at lunch talking to a heart surgeon. I asked what he found to be the greatest hindrance to good health. He responded that many people are unwilling to change. He stated that even after getting a diagnosis of ill health and being told that certain changes were needed, many would continue with the same behavior even though it meant destroying their health. He said some people ended up getting limbs cut off rather than changing their habits and behavior.

A number of people say they want to move beyond their adversity, but they are so afraid of change so they continue with the same life style even though it is destroying them. So many people would rather be destroyed than change. Do you know that if you place a frog in water and turn up the heat gradually the frog will sit in the boiling water and die? Many people are like that frog. The water or situation is getting hotter, but they continue to sit there and are ultimately destroyed.

I remember reading about a professor who had a six-figure income, but because of adversity in her life she jumped from a six-story building to her death. So often it is not the problem but how we approach or perceive the problem that makes the difference. If we are going to make it through adversity, we cannot be afraid of the unknown or of doing something different. Hebrew 11:1 "Now faith is the substance of things hoped for and the evidence of things not seen." We need to take a careful look at that word <u>substance</u>. In Greek, it is <u>hupostases</u>, made up of stasis (to stand) and hupo (under); in other words, "that" which stands "under" a foundation. It defines the ground on which one builds one's hope.

You need a firm foundation. For example, quicksand might seem to be firm but a person can find himself in a life threatening situation because the foundation is not firm. If you are going to build a home that can withstand storms, it needs a good foundation. Faith is the title-deed of the things hoped for. For example, let's say there is a car in California at the dealership and you have not seen it. But when you go to the dealership and present the title-deed you are able to drive away with the car because you have shown ownership although you had never seen the car before.

"Faith is the assurance of things hoped for. It is the firm grasp of faith on unseen fact" (Vincent). This is not a contradiction. No matter how dark it got, he continued to have faith. You must also have faith if you are going to survive your crisis. It is darkest before dawn, the same way as in life it can be very dark before a breakthrough. The battle for our survival will be fought in our mind. What is most important is our self-talk. Everyone has a conversation with oneself, and the self-talk will determine the outcome of our life. If you tell yourself that you cannot make it through, you will not. Your self-talk is very important. I had a nervous breakdown in part because of self-talk. I kept telling myself that I would not be able to come out of this situation because it was so bad.

What kind of self-talk are you having with yourself? The dialogue we have between our two ears or in our mind is vitally important. We have to be careful what kind of thoughts we dwell on. This is not discussed often, but it is very important. Our very survival during difficult times is determined by our self-talk. We cannot control every thought that comes through our mind, but we can decide what we dwell on. I heard an example given once: that you cannot stop a bird from flying over your head, but you can stop it from making a nest there.

It is our perception of a situation that determines if we will make it through. You can find two people in the same dilemma. One will survive and one may not because of how they look at the same situation. For example, two people can be told by the doctor that they have a terminal illness and have six months to live. One person may believe the doctor and live six months, and the other person may not believe the doctor and live many years.

I do not recall where I read this, but it stated, "You can believe the diagnosis but not the prognosis." The doctor may say you have a certain illness and you may need to change your life style. Earvin "Magic" Johnson was told he had HIV. Many people with HIV are dead after a few years, but "Magic" made certain changes, and he is living a very productive life. He has started a number of businesses. He did not deny the diagnosis; he just did not accept the prognosis. Magic said he does not focus on death but on enjoying life. My point is, do not let your current situation fool you into giving up on life.

You must control your thought pattern if you are going to make it through the difficulties in life. "When you get into a tight place and everything goes against you, and it seems as though you could not hold on a moment longer, never give up then, for that is just the place and time that the tide will turn," observed Harriet Beecher Stowe. Those that overcome will receive the keys to life. I was listening to an audio book by Dr. Robert Schuler entitled "Turning Hurts into Halos and Scars to Stars." It reminded me that sometimes when looking back on hurts, they do not seem quite as bad. A Chinese proverb states, "We need to wait five minutes to see if it is a blessing or a curse." There is something you might feel is a curse today, but later on you may consider it a blessing.

The idea for this book came from a one-minute speech I gave at a Les Brown seminar. In my presentation I stated that if Mr. Brown had not achieved success through adversity, he would not be living his current life. If you find yourself in a bad situation, you must continue to remind yourself that it will not last always. I remember early in my ministry going through some difficult times, and I asked my pastor, at the time Reverend Jeremiah Blow, why am I going through this? He simply asked me, "Why not you? What makes you so special you should not go through hard times?" Everyone will have his or her share of hard knocks.

Achieving Success Through Adversity

Earl Nightingale, the great motivational speaker, said "our attitude will determine our altitude in life." In his tape on attitude, he told about a great chef who had slept on park benches for many years. He was asked when he had become a success. He responded, "In my mind I was always a success even though I was sleeping on a park bench." Because we must think it before we can see it. The Wright brothers were bicycle makers. They saw the airplane flying in their mind first. I have read about men who have been shipwrecked. The young men died at a much higher rate than the older men did. It was attributed to the fact that the older men had been in shipwrecks before, and so they did not panic. As it is in life, once God has brought us through a difficult time we have a reference point to look back on.

I had a health crisis and was sitting in the doctor's office. It was a beautiful summer day and I looked up at the top of the trees from the chair I was sitting in. I thought about what God had already brought me through, and I remembered the scripture that said if I take the wings of a dove, I will meet God in the sky; and if I make my bed in hell, God is there. In other words, God is omnipresent. There is no situation where God is not available. We must access the power. It is available to us if we so choose.

The story was told once of an area that did not have electricity. They installed electricity in all of the homes. After checking the peoples' electric bills, they wondered why one old lady's bill was so low. They went to discuss it with the senior. She stated that at night she used candles instead of the electric power. The power was available, but she just did not use it. The power of faith is available to us, but we must use it.

Chapter Two

We Need to Be True to Ourselves

"Being myself includes taking risks with myself, taking risks on a new way of being myself, so that I can see who it is I would be."

Hugh Prather

WE NEED TO BE TRUE TO OURSELVES

We can be dishonest with others, but we should be true to ourselves. We should spend many hours, days, months, and years finding out who we really are. I do not believe a person can achieve any lasting success unless that person really knows himself. James Allen, in his great book entitled As A Man Thinketh, states that circumstances only reveal what is really going on inside a person. Allen says the circumstance only reveals the seeds of thought that have been planted in the mind. Nelson Mandela was released after 27 years in prison, but he did not come out bitter. Because of his attitude, South Africa did not fight a civil war when he was released. The country was not in turmoil from people trying to exact revenge because they had been mistreated.

In As A Man Thinketh, James Allen goes on to state that we can assume a good person suffers because of goodness and a bad person prospers from illegal activity. We cannot really know until we understand the thoughts within the person whether one suffers because of goodness and the other prospers because of illegal activity. Earl Nightingale's famous speech "The Strangest Secret" implies that we become what we think, whatever is our dominant thought: "As a man thinketh in his heart . . . " I was telling a young man sometime ago when I decided to discover who I really was, I thought it would take a few days but I discovered it took many years to find out. It seems that so many people live in a state of denial. We will not make any progress in our life until we take a self-evaluation of our strengths and weaknesses. When we begin to take a serious look at ourselves, we are probably going to find some things we do not like that are going to be hard to change.

During interviews, I like to ask people what their strengths and weaknesses are. I believe the response can tell you a lot about a person. I remember interviewing a person, and I asked the question, "Do you have any weaknesses?" The response was, "I do not have any at all." This person was probably 150 pounds overweight, but the response was she did not have any weaknesses. If we do not acknowledge and face our problems, we will not be able to make any improvements. We must know our strengths and weaknesses. Not that I would necessarily tell the world about my weaknesses, but I need to acknowledge them to myself.

There is no way we can successfully navigate through life without really knowing ourselves. We should not pursue our dreams only because that is what someone else wants for our life. If our life is going to be fulfilled, we must decide what we really want and not let other people dictate what our life pursuit should be. Sometimes it can be painful when we take an honest look at ourselves. There may be some things in our past that we regret. We all know that we cannot change the past, but hopefully we can learn from it and have a better future and not continue to make the same mistakes.

To get to really know yourself you need to be able to spend time alone. Ask yourself many questions. For example, why am I going in this particular direction? Do I realize I need to make certain changes, but I am afraid because I do not know what the future will bring? As I mentioned, it was not easy finding out who I was. Sometimes to get to know who you are, you may have to deal with some heartaches and disappointments from your past. The old saying from when I was a kid, "Sticks and stones may break my bones, but names will never hurt me," is a lie from the pit of hell.

There are some things said that take people a lifetime to get over. Maybe someone who should have loved you and encouraged you, put you down and told you that you never would amount to anything. That is not an easy thing to overcome, but if you are going to have a successful and peaceful life you must find a way to put it behind you. Sometime we may need to talk to a good friend, but we must be sure it is someone we can really trust to hold in confidence what we share.

I remember many years ago during a very difficult time in my life when I told a friend of a private and serious issue I was going through. Someone called from out of town and said he did not know I was going through such an experience. I told only one person, but eventually it went not only all over town but across the United States! Be careful in whom you confide. Being true to oneself does not mean everyone will necessarily approve. That does not mean it is good or bad. We need to realize when we self-actualize that not everyone is going to approve of the person we have become.

Dr. A. H. Maslow studied a number of people including Albert Einstein, Eleanor Roosevelt, and Frederick Douglass. Dr Maslow describes the steps a person goes through to self-actualize. The steps include: physiology, safety, love and belonging, self-esteem, and self-actualization. When you become a self-actualized person, you know who you are — the good, the bad, etc. I am a fairly confident person, for example, but some people perceive me as being arrogant. However, I would not let that change me from being who I am just because everyone does not approve. What kind of self-image do you have? We get our self-image from our experiences in life. Quite often they develop during childhood from the good things and bad things that happen to us.

Maxwell Matz, a plastic surgeon, wrote the book <u>Psycho Cybernetics</u>, in which he relates a story of a beautiful young woman who was in a car accident. Her face was repaired by surgery. Dr. Matz asked her how she liked her new face. She stated that she did not notice any changes at all. Dr. Matz realized that we have an inner picture of ourselves, a self-image. You will never have peace without a good self-image. Without a good self-image you will not overcome adversity and experience greatness. The good thing about self-image is that it can be changed.

Our nervous system does not know the difference between what is actually happening and what we are imagining in our mind. Therefore, if the situation is not real, we can create it (synthetically) with our thoughts. We can visualize a situation in our mind and begin to walk through it in a quiet place without distraction. I am not trying to say we can just imagine all our problems away without doing anything, but we can develop more confidence by seeing ourselves taking specific action before we encounter the actual situation. As far as our nervous system is concerned we have already gone through it. Whatever we imagine in vivid detail, our nervous system believes we have already experienced it. However, we must be willing to take action, which is not always easy to do. We do not like it but it takes pressure sometimes to bring about change.

As noted earlier, to get a diamond from a piece of coal requires immense pressure. When you first look at a piece of coal you probably never imagine it could become a beautiful diamond. Some of us are like that piece of coal with a diamond inside, and the only way to get the diamond out is to apply pressure. Once we come through adversity we are stronger and better. When a refiner takes gold and silver ore out of the ground it has a lot of dirt on it. He places it into a refiner's bowl and turns up the heat to eliminate the dirt and filth. Sometimes it takes the heat in our life to burn away some of the negative things in our life. Heat is a preserver, not a destroyer.

When I was a young boy, my mother would can preserves: apples and peaches. She would cut away the rotten spots and place them in a tin pan in the oven and turn on the heat. After a period of time she would take them out and put them in a canning jar with a tight lid and place it on the shelf. Months later we would get the preserves off the shelf and eat them, and they were very good. What had preserved them was the heat.

We should not let anything get inside our minds and cause turmoil in our lives. If we do not deal with the struggle from within, we will be destroyed. I recall a story told once of a beautiful butterfly. It is said that a little boy saw a butterfly struggling to get out of the cocoon and eventually it flew away.

Achieving Success Through Adversity

The butterfly starts its life as a caterpillar that crawls through the mud. When I was a kid the caterpillar was repulsive to me. I did not realize that a beautiful butterfly had been a caterpillar that had made a transformation. The caterpillar has to eat the right kind of leaves to spin the cocoon that would hold the larva.

If we do not eat the right kind of foods and keep the right thoughts inside of us, we will be destroyed. The little boy saw how the previous butterfly had struggled to get out of the cocoon, so he decided to help the next butterfly. He took a pin and opened the cocoon so the butterfly would not have to struggle. He anticipated that the beautiful butterfly would just fly away. Instead, it hit the ground and was unable to fly away. Later, someone explained to the young man that it was good for the butterfly to struggle to get out of the cocoon. Struggling pushed fluid to the butterfly's wings which enabled it to fly. So actually the struggle was beneficial.

So it is with us humans. Struggles help us define who we are. Knowing who you are does not mean that every step one is going to take everyone will say yes, continue your course. For myself, I sometimes have to look for a higher power to provide comfort for the direction of my life. I cannot emphasize enough the importance of spending time alone to gather your thoughts and come to the realization of who you are. I do not know how a person can really have a full life without knowing oneself. If you know you are living your life in the right way, but no one else agrees, you should continue your course. It does not mean being stubborn and continuing what you know deep down inside is wrong, while showing people you do not have to change. If you continue in that process you will live to regret it.

We Need to Be True to Ourselves

The only way you will be able to withstand difficult times is to know who you are. You must evaluate whether criticism of you is right or wrong. Life will challenge you, and you need to be secure enough to stand when the winds of adversity blow on you. What is my purpose in life? If you know your purpose, you can better understand who you are, or who you should be. To know myself will help me when it seems like I am going through life all alone. We will have periods when it seems hard to find someone who understands our dilemma. If we live a life of lies, we will never be happy. As painful as the truth is, life will be better living a life of truth. I want you to ask yourself again, "Who am I?" Not who I am pretending to be, but who I really am.

We can all change, but we must be honest concerning our current situation. Once we determine who we are, we can pinpoint the areas that need improvement. There is no way to become the person we each need to be without being honest with oneself. Often we have to look back on a situation to see its value, because when we are going through the situation we cannot always see its value. If we are going to be true to ourselves, we must be honest no matter how painful it might be. Unless we have accurate appraisals of ourselves, we will not be able to achieve our goals. We must be able to accept constructive criticism.

For example, I was looking to improve my public speaking skills. A few people mentioned I had a tendency to speak too fast. I could ignore that criticism, but I would never go to another level. If we are not true to ourselves, we will never improve. It is not being like anyone else because there is a divine plan for each of us. We should learn from other people, but also be original. There is nothing as strong as the original. There is no stronger copy than the original. I see so many people trying to be like someone else.

Some people live their lives through watching television. They sit and watch as their lives slip away. I took a personality test that pointed out many of my strong points and some that could be perceived as weak points. It gave me considerable information concerning myself as well as information on how to navigate through life. It is difficult sometime to accept negative points about ourselves. But if we are going to know ourselves, we must accept the good and the bad. We need to evaluate and determine if it is good or bad. For instance, the evaluation said some might perceive me as a perfectionist. I do not see that as a problem because I believe as professionals we should do things to the best of our ability. We should strive for perfection. Some individuals may be critical but I will not allow that to stop me.

If one is true to oneself, a person needs to listen to uplifting material. We might need to listen to motivational tapes and read books of the same nature. We need to keep reinforcing the positive. During difficult times, it is important to keep positive information flowing into one's mind. In a split second, one can make the wrong decision. That is why it is so important to have positive information in your mind. It is important not to let someone else dictate what your life should be, or what goals you should set. Sometimes people are so concerned about what other people may think they do not strive to achieve their dream.

I find this quite often with young people. Because a friend does not want to do anything positive, a youth decides not to strive for his or her goal. To be true to yourself, you must realize not everyone you meet will go through your entire life's journey

We Need to Be True to Ourselves

with you. There may be some people you would very much like to go with you, but when you go to another level the altitude may be too high for them.

Many years ago I wanted to start a business with a friend. I stated I could get a loan from the Veterans Administration to expand the business. That friend could not see beyond the small business concept; he could not see the potential for a much larger enterprise. After a period of time I came to realize that I needed to be true to myself. For what I wanted to do with my life, that friend could only be a small part of my journey. As I look back on those years, that person has not come close to his potential. If we are going to be true to ourselves, we cannot be afraid of change. We can stay on the pier and hope to catch bundles of fish, but at some point we must be willing to launch out into the deep. We need to take calculated risks.

We should not start out on a course without planning. I cannot emphasize enough the importance of faith. I will cite an example: to determine if you really have faith, you can see a boat sailing, and you can say I believe that boat will take me to my destination, but faith is not shown until one is willing to get on the boat to sail to the port. We need to be secure in ourselves to walk it alone; we must be willing to do that. There will be those moments when it seems no one understands but we need to know ourselves well enough to say I would like you to understand and agree, but if you do not, I know my destiny, and I must continue the course that I have charted for my life. I do not mean anyone should be stubborn and refuse wise counsel, but you have to understand that not everyone always understands.

There are countless stories of people who have achieved

great things, when many loved ones thought they were making a big mistake. The others could not possibly see because it was not their vision. I am sure many people have missed out on their dreams because when they took a survey others did not agree with them. Being true to myself means that even if no one else understands I must do what I believe is best for me. That is why it is important to know yourself so that when the dark days come and it is hard to find a friend with enough courage to stay the course, you will not be deterred. If you do not really understand who you are and your purpose when times get tough and the doubters come out of the woodwork you will miss your destiny. It would be nice to have someone give encouraging words but that might not happen.

Mahatma Gandhi was a major political and spiritual leader of India and the Indian independence movements for civil rights and freedom across the world. In India, Mahatma Gandhi is officially accorded the honor of Father of the Nation, and his birthday, October 2nd, is commemorated each year as Gandhi Jayanti Day, a national holiday. On June 15, 2007, the United Nations General Assembly unanimously adopted a resolution declaring October 2nd to be the "International Day of Non-Violence" (Wikipedia, the free encyclopedia). If Gandhi had not been committed to his purpose he would not have realized his true destiny. Gandhi endured much criticism, but he was secure in his mission. If we are going to realize greatness we must be willing to withstand criticism. Gandhi never had 100 percent of the people of India in support of his ideas but he was not deterred.

Sometimes adversity prepares us for our ultimate mission in life. Most normal people do not enjoy such preparation. I have said many times that we have to look back on a situation to see its value. In the midst of it, we cannot see any possible good that could come out of the situation. In the midst of our troubles, if we can work our way through the maze, there is a potential for greatness. We cannot always know when our dream will manifest. I said I wanted to be a director of an agency in 1985, but it did not happen until 2003. There are times when I felt sure that I had reached my goal only to be disappointed. I remember so clearly at one point when I had gotten all excited because I was getting ready to see my dream fulfilled, but I was sadly mistaken.

I was sitting at home and feeling dejected when I got word that I had not gotten the job. When I was able to look back on the situation, I realized it was not the best time for me. Had it happened earlier, I would have been like a puppet on a string. I believe God did not let it happen sooner because it was not best for me. Many years later when I became an executive director, I was much better prepared to lead the organization. I was a more mature and knowledgeable person at that point in my life. I was better able to navigate through the politics required to lead an agency. Sometimes before a big breakthrough it may seem as if we are at our lowest point. Because we cannot see everything, it does not mean the universe is not bringing the dream together.

A good example that comes to mind is the Moonflower. This flower only blooms in the evening. There are 4- to 6-inch large fragrant white or pink flowers on the twisting vines. The flowers open quickly in the evening, last through the night, and remain open until touched by the morning sun. Moonflowers grow to a height of 15 feet. The flower does not grow during sunlight but during the onset of evening. So we too might not get many accolades, but we can still move toward our goal. We may not be in the sunlight or spotlight, but we should still move in the right direction. We must be self-assured during tough times and have enough courage and patience to stay the course.

CHAPTER THREE

DO NOT PLAY THE BLAME GAME

"Each player must accept the cards life deals him. But once they are in hand, he alone must decide how to play the cards in order to win the game."

Voltaire

DO NOT PLAY THE BLAME GAME

Some people blame others for the conditions they find themselves in. Each person must decide to take responsibility for his/her own life. What Voltaire states is true. Life deals each one of us certain cards, and we must decide how we will play the hand that has been dealt us to win the game.

I was talking to my friend Rene Godefroy, and he questioned why I chose to deal with the subject of adversity. I answered that when people are going through difficult times they do not see the value, nor do they realize that the difficulty may turn out to be a blessing. I said to him, for example, think of when you were young living in Haiti in poverty and was very sick. When you were going through that experience, you were not thinking that I will grow up, become a motivational speaker, and this experience will be of great benefit to me. However, I told Rene, your success has been achieved through your adversity. It has turned out to be a blessing because that experience opened many doors for you.

We must hold on to our faith. The only thing that is going to get us through difficult times is our faith. Often we blame others rather than take responsibility for our life. We must decide what changes are necessary to make our situation better. All the crying and complaining will not make life better. When I find myself in a difficult situation, I think, "What is my plan?"

I will never forget Mr. Eugene Fisher, a great mentor, who was previously the Board Chair of MOCAP, Inc. I was discussing with him the numerous problems ahead and what needed to be done to make sure the agency I was directing would survive. He asked me, "If you were going to eat an elephant, how would you go about it?" I responded that I would eat it one bite at a time. To solve a problem, we need a system to break the problem into parts. Mr. Fisher believed in me when there were many doubters.

Mr. Eugene Fisher,
Former Board Chair of MOCAP, Inc. & Mentor

Do Not Play the Blame Game

I decided if the agency was going to survive, I needed to get some help to identify and implement the necessary changes. I contacted David Bradley, CEO for the National Community Action Foundation, and he referred me to management consultants, H&D Associates, Robert Halsch and Allan DeGiulio. They were able to help me navigate the agency through a very difficult transition.

When you find yourself in difficult times, you often need to ask for help. No one person knows everything. Many people do not ask for help when they find themselves in a difficult situation. If they had asked for help, they might have found a solution. You cannot expect other people to do everything for you, but when you have done all that you can there is nothing wrong with asking for help.

Unfortunately, Mr. Fisher died before we completed the difficult transition. I asked Bishop Nathan Wells to be chairman, and he gave great leadership in helping lead the agency out of trouble. Bishop Wells is still a great friend whom I still call to get wise counsel. You cannot sit back and wish yourself through difficult times, you must take action. There were some people on the board who were determined to terminate me. However, no one can derail your purpose. As difficult as it may be, if you do what is right and do not get what you want, then it was not meant for you. It was not in God's plan.

We need to make sure that we have done everything we can do. If it means burning the midnight oil late into the night to solve your problems, you must be willing. You might need additional education to help you achieve your goals. Sometimes you need to change the people with whom you surround yourself. During difficult times, you need to associate with positive people. For example, my wife's niece, Toni was diagnosed with breast cancer, and her so-called friends said it was terminal. However, Toni kept a good attitude and was determined to survive the illness to live a positive and productive life. If she had believed what her friends said, her life would have been over. Words of encouragement are nice, but they may not always come when we want them. We must find something within ourselves.

My wife, Betty Mae, told me a few days ago that a former member of the church I had been the pastor of was telling people that I am arrogant. She was reluctant to tell me because she felt it would hurt my feelings. I told her my feelings were not hurt because I am confident, not arrogant. A person needs to be secure in the person that he or she is even though others may not understand. If you are going to accomplish anything in life, you must have confidence.

I heard the great authors Mark Victor Hansen and Jack Canfield say that over 140 people rejected the idea for their book, "Chicken Soup for The Soul." Subsequently, they have made millions of dollars and many doors of opportunity have opened for them. What if they had conceded because people did not think it was a good idea? They would not be living the lives they have now. Do not feel bad about things over which you have no control, because you cannot control everybody's comments. I do not mean you should be arrogant and mean but you should persist in your own vision.

Do not let others destroy your self-image. Even your relatives sometimes can be "haters." You must protect your positive self-image and not give your own power over to someone else. I

Do Not Play the Blame Game

want people to like me, but I understand no matter what I do, everyone is not going to like me. It is not possible for everyone to like you. I came to that realization when I was in high school. There were certain people that did not like me, and that bothered me. When I thought about it, I realized that I had done nothing wrong to them. They just did not like me. Some people will dislike you just because you are successful. Some people will dislike you just because their own life is miserable. Additionally, sometimes the old saying is true: Misery loves company.

My time had eventually come, and I assumed the leadership of our agency. I am glad to say the agency is doing well and we have been able to add millions of dollars to our current budget.

One of the problems that stops people from getting beyond substance abuse is they think about how hard it is to quit forever, rather than thinking I am going to promise myself not to indulge for a few hours. The short breaks can lead to a lifetime of sobriety. I thank God I have common sense. If you look at a problem from three points of view and eliminate two, you may arrive at the right answer. I call it the <u>triangle effect</u> because a triangle has three sides. You must be determined to make lasting change. It does not do you any good to talk about change and continue doing things the same way. Talk alone will not do. Many times, we are not honest with ourselves and admit we caused the problem.

When I was in high school, I did not plan to go to college. I had planned to be a great hustler, so I did not need to go to college to carry out that plan. I also did not like English during high school so I avoided taking the subject after it was no longer required. I ended up going into the United States Air

Force because for a period of time I could not find a job. After completing my tour with the Air Force, I qualified for a college education through the G. I. Bill.

One of the requirements to get a Liberal Arts Degree was to pass an English course. The first paper I got back from the instructor was so full of red, it seemed as if it should be on its way to the emergency room. I complained about how difficult the instructor was, but the real reason was that I did not prepare myself in high school. I wanted to blame the instructor, but it was my fault. Sometimes, when we experience difficulties, we believe the problem is only unique to us, but it really is not. A circumstance you do not like can turn out to be a blessing.

All of the individuals that I have studied who have documented great accomplishments have done so by overcoming setbacks and disappointments. Your great accomplishment is on the other side of the problem you might be facing currently. There is greatness waiting for us once we are willing to face our obstacles and fears. The victory is ours, but we must be willing to face the giants that will come up against us. I heard actress Kim Basinger say something I found to be profound. She said that whenever she faced fear, "I do the opposite of what fear is telling me to do." What stops a person from achieving a goal is the fear of failure.

Fear is a powerful emotion. I was watching television one night in a hotel, and a program came on explaining the effects of stress. A mother, after an x-ray uncovered a scar on her lungs, just knew it was cancerous and thought she would not be able to see her daughter get married. She became so sick that they were not sure she would live. After the tests were finally done, it was determined that the scar was benign. It was not cancerous, but because the woman believed so strongly that it was cancer, it had almost killed her.

The mind is very powerful. The only way to protect it is through your thoughts. Fear is false information appearing to be real. Whatever fear you are dealing with as far as the body and nervous system are concerned is often perceived and accepted as real. This woman almost died because of fear. They call it <u>broken heart syndrome</u>. She believed so strongly it almost killed her. Sometimes fear looms so big in our lives we cannot do anything.

Fears are sometimes like shadows. I preached a message entitled "Shadows." One day I was preoccupied with thinking as I was walking down the stairs into my basement to retrieve something from the dryer. A huge figure startled me, and I began to move back. Once I shifted my position, I realized I was about to run from my own shadow, which had seemed big and menacing. Some things we fear are only shadows or illusions. Shadows come in different sizes and shapes in accordance with the object in front of the light or sun. When you see a shadow, it does not mean the sun has stopped shining. The sun is only blocked by an object.

It is said that Alexander the Great had a horse that was so afraid of his shadow that no one could ride it. Alexander made the horse face the sun (or its problem), and the horse was able to carry Alexander to many victories. In fact, Alexander the Great conquered the entire Greek world. You cannot run away from your fears. At some point you must face them. Sometimes fear freezes us. If we only shift our position, we would find out that it is not as bad as we thought. We need to evaluate the situation to see if we need to make changes.

If you keep doing things the same way as you have always done, you will keep getting what you have always gotten. Instead of blaming others, you need to chart a new course out of the situation. If the situation is not what you want, you must imagine in your mind the situation you want to create. It will not help you to sit back and have a pity party about how bad life is. Quite often, we learn more from our failures than we do from our successes. Our failures make us stop and evaluate our life. Sometimes we have to fail our way to success!

People young and old check out of life because they feel despair. But there is always hope because circumstances in life are like the seasons of the year. Anyone who lives in a region with different seasons realizes that there are spring, summer, fall, and winter. Sometimes in our life we experience all the seasons. No matter what season you are in, even if it is winter, do not give up because that season will change in due time. We must look within ourselves and to God to uplift our lives or spirits. If by chance we make a mistake, it is like a compass that helps us chart a new course for our life. If we play the blame game, it will not really help us to move forward. If everything you say is true about what someone may have done to you, what difference is it going to make? I am not making light of your problem, but you must realize that complaining will not make any difference.

The following is a true story. There was a lady who was sexually abused by her father. After years of distress from it and then having half her stomach cut out because of the stress, she realized that if she was going to survive, she had to let it go. Her experience was true, and it was devastating to think that person who should have protected her was her molester. However, she reached a point in her life when she knew she had to let this go. Even if you are totally right about being mistreated, you have to leave it behind and move forward.

I am thankful that my mother, Ida B. Shelton, really believes in God and in the importance of living according to the principles of Christianity. She often talked to me about how important it is to forgive. If we do not forgive, it does more harm to us than the person who has done us wrong. It is not always what a person eats that hurts him or her, but what is eating him or her. Making excuses will not help us have a peaceful life or achieve our goals in life. Each one of us must take responsibility for our own life. You must have determination that you are going to make whatever changes are necessary for you to have a better life. Some people think so much about how bad life is that they do not take time to think about a plan for changing their situation.

A man named Vick was working on a cooler and believed he had locked himself in the cooler. He kept getting colder and colder. After some time, he decided to write a letter to his loved ones because it had become so cold that he feared he would die. He froze to death. They found him the next day hard as a rock, frozen to death. But after carefully checking, they discovered that the cooler system was not working. He had created the whole situation in his mind. Fear is a powerful emotion.

Rather than blame others, we must take responsibility for our life. Whatever situations we find ourselves in are the consequences of the decisions we have made. If we find ourselves in good situations, most likely we made good choices, and if not, we made bad decisions. Instead of blaming others, we need to chart a course out of the situation. If the situation is not what we want, we must imagine in our mind the situation we want to create.

You cannot change the past, but, hopefully, you can learn and have a better future. I cannot emphasize enough the importance of forgiving. As I have mentioned, if someone has done us wrong, we need to reach a point of forgiveness. It is important what we eat, but sometimes what eats at us can be more damaging than what we have eaten. If we keep within us hate and stress, it will destroy us from within. Therefore, forgiveness is not so much for the person that has wronged us but is good for our own well-being.

Chapter Four

Do You Really Want Success?

"History has demonstrated that most notable winners usually encountered heartbreaking obstacles before they triumphed. They won because they refused to become discouraged by their defeat."

B. C. Forbes

Do You Really Want Success?

Some say they want success but keep doing things the same way they have always done and expect to get different results. When I was a pastor I observed many people who only came to church when they had a problem. If you are going to have any success, you need to be consistent. Success leaves footprints. If someone walks in the snow before you, he leaves his footprints. There are certain things you must do if you hope to succeed. You need to make the right decisions. I am not saying that anyone can live a life without making mistakes, but you should always try to do what is right.

Life is like a chess game, and you will enjoy or suffer the consequences of your decisions. You might have looked the board over and thought of a good move. It turned out to be the wrong move, and you will have to suffer the consequences of your decision, adjust and move in a different direction. When you go to college, you have to pay tuition, and that is the way of life. Sometimes life requires that we pay. Sometimes you pay in money, and sometimes you pay with heartache and disappointment. To get the diploma of life requires that you pay your dues.

I was talking to Gerald Stewart, a friend of mine, who revealed that at one time he was addicted to crack cocaine. He realized that to break the addiction, he had to move out of the house and away from the people who were using crack. He told the guys who were using not to come around him, and he has been off crack for a number of years now. He found success because he was willing to do something different. If you want success, there are some toxic people you need to stay away from.

If someone always brings you bad news, you do not need to be around that person. This point was brought home to me in a big way. I went to a wonderful conference given by Mark Victor Hansen. A lady sitting at a table began to complain about the lunch. I was thinking about all the good information I had heard. I never gave the meal much thought because I was there to learn. Her comments were poisonous to the environment. Here we have a person at a motivational conference who is very negative. It reminded me how important it is to avoid constantly negative people.

We should be conscious of the aura we give off. In other words, what kind of attitude do we have? A flower can give off a beautiful scent. Do we have a positive or negative aura? It is one thing to say you want success but another thing to do something really significant in your life. It is easy to talk about change. Talk requires no effort. It is similar to the person who says they want to lose weight but keeps eating three donuts a day. That person is not serious about wanting to change his life. It is only talking.

Do You Really Want Success?

We must hold a vision of what we want to create. I heard a story about a prince with a hunchback. A short time before the prince's birthday, his father, the king, asked the young man what he wanted for his birthday. The prince replied, "I want a statue of myself in the garden that I can see every day." The king thought the son was trying to mock him. The son said, "Father, I do not want a statue of myself as I am now but a statue of what I am going to become." Each day the prince would get up and look at the statue in the beautiful garden and then stretch and move. Eventually, he began to look like the statue. He was transformed because he held a vision of what he wanted to become. However, you need to make sure you have thought about it, and you are making the right decision.

The book <u>Think and Grow Rich</u> by Napoleon Hill states that sometimes you need to put yourself in a situation that precludes your turning around. I disliked my factory job, and each night as I entered the building, I began to shake because of nervousness. I decided I needed to find something different to do. I had the G. I. Bill to pay for my education so I quit my job and went back to school full time. Failing was not an option because I had quit my job. I had to get that liberal arts degree. I also had a family to care for so there was no turning back. I had a G. I. allowance coming in each month to help pay the bills so I had an effective plan.

I heard Les Brown observe that many people die on Monday morning because they hate going to their jobs. One day at a conference I was sitting next to an acquaintance, and she mentioned that a friend of hers was going to a job he did not like on Monday morning and died of a heart attack. I told her what Mr. Brown had said. Certainly, we cannot immediately quit every job we do not like, but we can make plans to find a more desirable job. We need to think it through. People make bad decisions and fail to take responsibility for landing in a bad situation. They blame everything and everyone but themselves. Sometimes we need to look at the person in the mirror.

I am reminded of another story that brings home the point that you have to be determined to succeed. I saw a true Hollywood story about the famous television cook Rachael Ray. Rachael revealed there were times when she was making only $50.00 for each episode and did not know how she was going to pay her rent, but she was persistent and kept performing her task to the best of her ability. Ms. Ray has an empire now because she would not quit. She also understands that not everyone is going to love her. When her life story was on television, it was revealed that a woman had started a Web page, "Rachel Ray Sucks." The woman disliked her because Rachel enjoyed laughing and body language, in other words the woman disliked Rachel because she was being herself.

About 6,000 other people also expressed their dislike for Ms. Ray on the website. They commented on how she dressed and gesticulated with her arms. Ms. Ray responded by saying she understood that not everyone is going to like her and that each person has that right. She did not get upset about what she could not control. When I got an opportunity to see the woman who started the Web page, I did not understand how this woman could criticize anyone. It seemed to me that this individual was very unhappy with her own life. If a person wants success, he or she should never forget that not everyone is going to like him or her.

I was watching the AFC championship game between the

Do You Really Want Success?

Indianapolis Colts and the New England Patriots in 2007. The score at half time was 21–3 in favor of the New England Patriots. I got upset because I wanted Coach Dungy to win. I was tired of hearing how he had never won the "big game." So I told my wife, Betty Mae, that the Colts would never climb back because they were playing against the great New England Patriots, an outstanding football team. When I complained about the score, Betty said the Colts could go into the locker room at half time, get energized, come back and win the game. I asked her if she really believed that. She said very calmly, "Yes, and they probably will come back and win." I did not believe it, so I switched the channel to something different, and I fell asleep.

I awoke about 11:30 pm and saw at the bottom of the screen: Colts 38, Patriots 34. I was reminded no matter what, we must hold on to our faith. Coach Dungy said during the first half when his team was down 21–3, "It is my time. I don't care what the score is now, it is still my time." The Colts not only won against the Patriots in the semi-finals they went on to win the Super Bowl against the Chicago Bears. We should have that same frame of mind no matter how dark or difficult the situation is: "It is still my time." We should continue to hold a mental picture of success no matter what the circumstances might imply.

I remember a few years ago a bank teller was fired for stealing from the bank where she worked. She took a polygraph test, and it indicated she was lying. The woman lost her job and went to jail. Her story was on television and the front pages of newspapers. Through it all, she continually said, "I did not steal the money." The polygraph said she was lying. Many people walked out on her and gave her no support. A year later, the money bag was found stuck in the money drop. No matter how apparent defeat might seem, we must not give up. It may be hard to find a sign that it is going to work out, but we have got to continue to believe. All things are possible to them that believe and polygraphs are not perfect.

As the great statesman Winston Churchill said, "Never give in. Never give in! Never give in. Never give in. Never, never, never, never give in! Nothing great or small, large or petty — never give in except to convictions of honor and good sense. Never yield to force. Never yield to the apparently overwhelming might of the enemy." We must never give up regardless of what appearances may suggest. We need to have mental toughness because it will determine what we do in life. We will not accomplish much with a weak mind. Sometimes there seems to be a long time of silence when nothing is happening, but we should continue to do what is right.

One test to determine how badly you want something is what you do when it is not happening as quickly as you would like. We should not judge by the rate of success of somebody else. We can look around and see someone else having great success, and we wonder why our life is not going the way we want. I heard Jackie Cooper, a car salesman in the tape series, "A Finishing Touch," who said something that was good to remember. He said that LUCK is Laboring Under Correct Knowledge.

If you want success, you must know your craft. It is necessary to get the education to help you achieve your goals. Jackie Cooper said that to be a good car salesman you need to know as much as you can about the car. He said that you should know the right location to show the car. You should also point out the beautiful amenities the car has, for instance, the interior, etc.

Do You Really Want Success?

I had to sell cars for a couple of years. It helped me provide for my children. I will never forget trying to sell a car. I had been selling cars because people liked me but not because I knew that much about the car. One day this very nice husband and wife that came to test drive a car. They could see I did not know that much about the car. The husband smiled and said, "Ken, you have got to learn more about the car." I knew he was right. After that, I started to learn more about the cars, and I turned out to be a pretty good car salesman.

On your way to success, you may have to take jobs you would not normally want to do. I told my oldest son, Ken Jr., "If you can stay afloat during difficult times, things can get better, but once you go under there is no hope." A person may fall off a boat, but if he has a flotation device, he can survive. There are incidents where someone has fallen off a boat accidentally and was able to survive because he had a life-jacket.

If you are going to be successful, you have to do whatever is necessary. I did not want to sell cars, but I had to take care of my family. There were times I had humiliating experiences. I had to bite my lip when I felt I was being treated unfairly. I do not mean you should allow someone to abuse you physically or totally destroy your self-image. The manager hollered at me once and said I had better get in the car and get out of there. It was not necessary for me to speak, but by the look I gave him, he knew I did not appreciate his manners. I got in the car because I could not indulge my pride. I had children depending on me. That experience of selling cars was good for my maturity. As an executive director, I am very conscious of how I treat individuals that work for me because I remember how I was treated when I was selling cars.

Achieving Success Through Adversity

If you are going to achieve success, everything will not go the way you want. You must adjust and make changes in accordance with unexpected circumstances. When you take a journey there are times you might miss the correct exit. If that happens, you must keep going until you find the right exit. So it is with life, you must keep working at it until you get the right formula for success.

I remember looking out my window as an Assistant Director for the Muskegon Heights Housing Commission and seeing the devastation wrought by crack cocaine. I saw very attractive women who had been destroyed in a matter of six months. I did not feel that I was doing anything worthwhile to address this problem, so I decided to quit and and start an agency with grant money for young people who were not living up to their potential. After about 10 months, the program was closed down, and I found myself selling cars. I never thought I would be a car salesman.

Life will throw you a curveball, and you will have to adjust. If you are to live a successful life, you need determination. Life will knock you down and bloody your nose. You must have determination no matter what is thrown at you. If you are determined, nothing will stop you from reaching your true destiny. It is important to keep feeding yourself positive information. There are so many negatives that come at us. We can get ten glowing compliments and one negative statement, but we focus on that one negative assessment. Instead of spending a lot of time thinking about the ten that approved of us, we focus on why one did not.

Our self-image is important. I remember watching a talk

Do You Really Want Success?

show. A DNA test was used to determine the father of a child. One woman said that whenever her son phoned his dad, he just hung up on the boy. I was thinking to myself, how stupid! Doesn't he realize he is destroying the kid's self-image. How is this kid going to feel good about himself when his earliest memory is of his father hanging up on him and not wanting to talk to him? The test proved that he was the boy's father. The moderator wondered why the woman would continue such a toxic relationship just because she wanted a family. No one should elevate anyone to such importance just to be with that person. I pray this kid will come out all right, but it is going to be tough.

Words can be like a self-fulfilling prophecy. Someone may say little Johnnie is no good, just like his father. That can be self-fulfilling. Sometimes we may need to find a coach. Tiger Woods is recognized as probably the greatest golfer in this era, yet, he has a coach. There are many star athletes who have coaches. Great singers and actors have coaches. How much do you really want success? Often there will be heartaches and disappointments in the pursuit of your dream. Your goal should not be an idle wish but what you really want. What do you have a strong passion for, that if you did not get paid you would continue to do? If I did not get paid to be an inspirational speaker, I would continue to speak because I believe it is important. I spend time speaking with youth at risk because it is my calling.

Our agency sponsors a program to inspire youth called "Empowering Our Youth." I had the idea probably ten years before I was able to implement the plan because the previous board did not think it was a good idea. However, I did not give up because I believed it was a great idea. For our first conference, I arranged to have the great motivational speaker Les Brown kick off the conference. It was a great success. I heard some educators say that one speech cannot make a difference. I do not believe that because one speech made a change in my life. It was the speech "I Have a Dream" by Dr. Martin Luther King, Jr. I remember one day running home to hear the speech. As I saw and heard the speech a tear ran down my face. That speech helped set the course for my life. We need a positive mental attitude (PMA).

Around 1979, I read Joe Karbo's book <u>Lazy Man's Way to Riches</u>. He stated that if his book was not worth at least a thousand dollars, the reader could return it and get a refund of the $10.00 book cost. I must admit it was worth far more than that to me. In fact, the information in that book has been worth hundreds of thousands of dollars to me. Karbo further stated that you must decide and focus on what you really want to do. You should not distract yourself with several different things. We must have a concrete plan: Read, Study, Visualize, and Perform (R. S. V. P.). We need to write down what we really want. We must put our own plan in motion.

So you say you want success. Success takes effort and correct planning. I say <u>correct planning</u> because a person can be sincerely wrong. Just because a person believes he is right does not make it so. If a person is going to be successful, there are questions he or she must ask him/herself. What am I committed to achieving? Because when times get tough, we need a compelling reason to stay the course. No one achieves success without time and effort, and you also need to surround yourself with positive people.

Mental toughness is also required to achieve success. What

Do You Really Want Success?

do I plan to give to realize my dream? You must decide what one thing you really want rather than a million different things if you are hoping to achieve your dream. What am I committed to achieving? Many times people say they want to accomplish specific objectives but do no want to put in time and effort to make it happen.

Success does not happen by accident. Each person must decide what success is. Someone might be quite happy being a teacher, a maintenance worker, or a crossing guard. That is okay. If you are doing what you really want to do, you are a success.

Chapter Five

The Power from Within

"You can conquer almost any fear if you will only make up your mind to do so. For remember fear doesn't exist anywhere except in the mind."

Dale Carnegie

THE POWER FROM WITHIN

You must look within yourself if you are hoping to reach your full potential. There is an orchard in every apple seed, but the ingredients within the seed must be released. The potential is there but if it is not released the orchard will never materialize. There is greatness in you, but you must release the power from within. Ralph Waldo Emerson said, "What lies before us is nothing compared to what lies within us." If we cut our hand, we do not have to say, "heal hand." There is something within us that will cause the cut to heal. You should look to within yourself to reach your destiny. The Planarian, or flatworm, can be cut in half and each cut section will develop into a new complete body. The front part organizes itself a new head, complete with brain, and the back part develops a new rear. The reason it is able to do this is because of the power from within.

I was watching the Power Rangers cartoon series with two of my grand-children, Cortez and Carlos, when one of the rangers said, "We must have courage if we are going to fulfill our destiny." This is so true. Many people are afraid to venture out to reach their goal because of the fear of failure. If you are going to achieve anything of significance, you must have courage. Thomas Edison, who had ten thousand failures before he invented the incandescent light bulb stated, "Our greatest weakness lies in giving up. The most certain way to succeed is always to try one more time."

Jim and Nell Hamm, husband and wife for 50 years, decided to go for a walk in Prairie Creek Redwoods Park. Nell stated they were walking in the forest discussing what a perfect day it was and how fortunate they were. It started getting dark and they decided to leave the park. Jim was walking behind Nell and heard something that he thought was someone on a bike. All of sudden life changed. Instead of a biker, he found himself face to face with a mountain lion. The lion attacked, Jim ducked and the lion flew over his head. But the lion was determined and swiftly came back and attacked him. Jim's life was in jeopardy. So it is with life sometimes. Things can be going well, but all of a sudden there is a shift, and you find yourself in the fight of your life. Just as Jim had to suddenly and unexpectedly fight for his life with the mountain lion, you have to fight to maintain when things shift. You cannot live in a lazy, carefree manner and think you will achieve your goals or successfully handle problems in your life.

Sometimes you are going to have to fight with everything that is within you. The mountain lion attacked Mr. Hamm; Jim said he had never fought a lion before but he did have experience with dogs. So he stuck his forearm in the lion's mouth. Hopefully, we can learn enough from past situations to help us deal effectively with our current issues. Nell turned around and saw the lion on top of Jim and she told him, "Jim, you got to fight."

The Power from Within

Do you have people around you that are encouraging or saying something negative? Not that you want only people around who say good things, but you do not want to be around people who are toxic. Eventually the lion got Jim's head in its mouth. The lion was trying to crush his skull. Jim said it would occasionally lick his skull. Nell grabbed a heavy wet log and thought that with one blow the lion would run away. But it did not. When we have problems in life if our plan does not work the first time, we must keep trying. Jim said he heard Nell saying again, "Jim you got to fight!" He asked himself, how can I fight with this lion on my back? The solution may not always come immediately but we must keep thinking of different ways to find the right answer. Nell saw something white on the ground and realized it was Jim's scalp. Sometime it can seem like life circumstances are trying to devour or destroy you. Jim's story says to me that when you are in a crisis, we need to keep our composure and we can make it through the crisis. If you panic you cannot think clearly how to navigate yourself out of the situation. Jim says he took his hand pushed the lion's nose back. The lion got very angry and tried to break Jim's neck.

Then Jim remembered from working with dogs that if he could grab the lion's tongue it would not be able to continue to bite him. So he realized that he could not do it for long but he could temporarily stop the lion from killing him. Sometime we must take a temporary solution. It will not be permanent fix, but it will help until you can figure out a better one. Then Jim took his fingers and stuck the lion in the eye, but it was relentless in its effort to kill Jim. During the attack, Jim told his wife very calmly to get the ball point pen and stab the lion in the eye. Nell said she kept hitting the lion until she felt she had no more strength, but decide to hit the lion one more time. With that strike, the lion ran away.

Sometimes, in life, you feel exhausted, but you must keep fighting even thought you are exhausted. If Nell had not struck the lion that one last time, her husband would have been devoured. How many people have missed a great opportunity because they did not try one more time? If her husband had not kept his composure, he would have been killed. In a difficult situation, he did not push the panic button. Imagine you are attacked by a lion and it is trying to kill you, even eat you. I find it amazing he was able to give his wife direction in that situation. It is vital to hold on to your composure. You must not allow stress to cloud your thinking if you are going to be successful.

Jim's story says to me that when we are in a crisis we must continue to fight the good fight of faith and never give up. Mrs. Hamm said it seems like it took ten years to get Jim loose from the lion and Jim said it seemed like forever. It is the same way with difficult times. Sometimes it seems to last forever but if you keep the faith, the storm will pass over. One of my favorite scriptures is I Corinthians 10:13 -"No temptation has seized you except what is common to man. And God is faithful; he will not let you be tempted beyond what you can bear. But when you are tempted, he will provide a way out so that you can stand up under it." Quite often in a crisis a person may feel that the situation is unique and that no one else has ever had to deal with something similar. The truth is that some will go through worse things and some will have lesser challenges. However, each one of us must fight our own battle to survive.

I know that when you are fighting your own battle it does not matter what someone else is going through. You are so preoccupied with getting through your crisis. You must remember you can only live one day at a time. The trouble comes when we try to live a multitude of days at once. Sometimes, you must say,

"I do not know what tomorrow will bring, but I am going to live with the events of the current day."

Many studies show that most people do not live up to their total potential. You must never forget that you have the power within to achieve your dreams and goals. If you can conceive and believe, you can achieve. Man has both a conscious and a subconscious mind. Whatever we constantly think in the conscious will eventually move to our subconscious. For example, have you ever prepared to pour something and think to yourself, I know I am going to spill this. Your hand trembled, and you did. Your subconscious reacted to the conscious thought. The subconscious has no limit other than what you place on it.

Robert Collier states in his book <u>The Secret of The Ages</u> that we have access to a universal mind, or what some might call a higher power. To Christians, it is Jesus Christ. The example Collier gives is that if you take a drop of water from the ocean, it is not as big as the ocean but it has all the ingredients of the ocean. He says it is the same with the Universal Mind. When you access it, your mind will not be as big, but it will have all the same elements. You must see yourself doing what you desire to do.

To be successful, you must have the right thought pattern. Quite often we paint over the masterpiece God has given us. We need to throw away the images that show poverty, or sickness, or unhappiness. We need to understand our heritage. I think many people have forgotten or do not realize they are made in the image of our God Almighty who created man and woman. God created man and woman in His own image. So when each one of us looks in the mirror, we see what God looks like because we are made in His image.

Psalm 139:14 states, "I will praise thee for I am fearfully and wonderfully made: your works are wonderful I know full well." Out of everything God created, nothing is as amazing as man and woman. The late Rev. E. V. Hill preached a sermon entitled "God Was at His Best When He Made Man and Woman." Wonderful, exciting wonder, marvelous, astonishing, a sight to behold, unusually good, incredible, amazing, fantastic, and phenomenal were the adjectives he used.

The reason it is important to discuss this is that many people are not living life to their full potential. You must visualize what you desire and claim it. Believe that you have it, and you will have it when you take the proper steps. Some people sit back, daydream, and hope that in some way success will just float into their lives. You must have a clear vision of what you want. You must visualize and claim it. You must also be willing to do what is required. You cannot sit back and wish for your dream to come to pass.

I recall reading that some people who watched the great movie "The Secret" believed they could just sit back and wish and their dream would come true as they sit on the couch. If you really want it, you have to go out and get it. We do not get from life what we idly wish for but what we aggressively go out and get. You must have the kind of determination to say that whatever it takes to achieve my goal, I will do. I was attending a Jim Rohn seminar and a gentleman sitting at my table was wearing an oriental outfit. I wondered why the man was wearing this outfit in America. Lying on our table was the book "Psycho-Cybernetics." The gentleman remarked in broken English that he had read the book and we began to talk. He indicated he had flown over 6,000 miles from Tokyo, Japan, to attend the seminar because he was seeking knowledge. On his business card was written, "Live everyday as a gift." We should live everyday as a gift because none of us knows how long we will be alive.

I remember hearing a young woman discuss how her mother wanted to write a book but became ill and was not able to finish the book. There is nothing more valuable than our time. What would most people give for more time at the end of their life? I have been fortunate to work with young men in our community. When I started, some acted as though they wanted to sleep, but I told them my time is too valuable to come there just for them to sleep. And I gave them a choice to either sit up and listen or to leave. We should not lose sight of the fact that our time is valuable. You can want so much for someone but if the person does not want it for himself, nothing significant will happen.

A truth is a truth whether we believe it or not. Many years ago, in 1976, after I got out of the United States Air Force, I remember what my instructor, Bob Hogan, told us in computer class. He said if we really learned about computers, we could provide a tremendous living for ourselves. My thought was that this guy is trying to trick us because no one wants to deal with these big computers. At that time, one computer would fill an entire room. There was no such thing then as a laptop computer. Bill Gates did not develop software for Microsoft until the mid 1980s. Fast forward many years and Gates is worth about $58 billion. Just because I did not believe what the instructor said did not stop it from being true.

You should live your life with truth being your guide. So often people live their life as pretenders. They think by pretending (lying to themselves) it will be true. If you are going to achieve anything, you should not make false promises to yourself. If you are going to achieve success regardless of adversity, there are some things you must be willing to give up. If a person wants a different life he or she must start doing things in a different way. To maintain motivation you must find it within yourself. You must have that spark within you, if you are going to achieve your dream. You must keep encouraging yourself during difficult times, because sometimes life can beat us up and knock us down.

Strength can be found deep within us. During hard times you must tell yourself, my day will come. Sometimes you set a goal hoping to achieve that goal within a certain time, but it does not always manifest when you would like. You can get discouraged when considering your life. You may have talents that have not been recognized. If a person is going to make it out of a difficult situation, he must believe things will get better. Many people feel they have been overlooked, become pessimistic, and throw in the towel.

Solomon tells us in Ecclesiastes 3:1–8: "There is a time and season for everything." Living in Michigan, we can, with a fair amount of accuracy, tell when one season ends and another begins. We know the cold or winter season will start around November or December and the spring season will start around March. When you are living your life you cannot always tell exactly when one season ends and another begins. Galatians 6:9 tells us, "And let us not be weary in well-doing: for in due season we shall reap, if we faint not." That is the key. Do not become weary doing what is right. Eventually we will benefit if we do not faint or give up.

Many people miss their blessing because they give up. Sometimes, our blessings may take days, months, and even years, but we must be willing to stay the course if we are doing what is right. Do not believe you are going to get the right results if you continue to do what is wrong. Negative actions or thoughts will never produce positive results. It is important to develop good habits. I heard it said that either you will make good habits or your habits will make you. Habits are powerful. If you usually put your right shoe on first, try to switch and put your left shoe on first. You will find that you almost automatically start to put the same shoe on that you have grown accustomed to putting on first.

I do not care what the present situation may be, you must hold a picture in your mind of the circumstances you want to create. You must keep preparing even though it might seem as if you are living a midnight situation during your everyday life. During difficult times, you must keep giving yourself the right self-talk. Tell yourself, "Although this situation is not what I want, I must keep doing what is right and hold on to my faith." Everything you receive will come through your faith. Faith can be used in a positive or negative way. If we believe something bad will happen, quite often it will. If you can hold on to your faith and believe something good will happen, eventually it will. As a Christian I believe that God has his own time, and He will bring me out if I continue to do what is right.

It is not always easy to do what is right, when it seems like everything is going wrong. I know this to be true: If you continue to do what is right, at some point you will be glad that you did and your situation will work out for the best. The only person you have control over is yourself. It is important that you keep yourself in the right frame of mind. Getting all upset because of what someone may or may not do will not do any good. It is important that I look within myself and make sure I am thinking right. I cannot emphasize enough the importance of self-talk. Are you saying positive or negative words to yourself? If it is not positive, you must change your self-talk.

Your thoughts will produce your reality. You should always monitor your internal conversation because you may not always have the right frame of mind and also because you can sometimes be unintentionally yet sincerely wrong just like anyone else. There have been times I thought about picking up an object, only to get to my destination and not have the object. But I searched for it because I was positive I had picked it up, only later to find out I had not, and it was in the very place I had seen it last.

I must emphasize the importance of being honest with yourself. It will not help you in your internal conversation to lie to yourself. Quite often a person will talk about doing something different with his life because he wants different things to occur, but he keeps doing things the same way as previously. How can that person really expect to get a different result? Whatever you do within your internal mind, there will be an outward manifestation.

I remember many years ago I had an opportunity to hear Pastor Donald Parson, a preacher who I loved to listen to. As I was sitting there preoccupied with my problems, a pastor I did not know came up to me and said, "What are you so worried about?"

I had not approached him to say I was worried, but he could

tell what was going on inside because there was a reflection of my thoughts on the outside. If you continue to poison your insides, it will become obvious to individuals everywhere, and it will break down your body.

I recently talked to an individual that had played an important role in my development as a man. My heart was very sad the other day when he called and talked with me. I could tell that drugs and alcohol had destroyed his mind. His conversation was way out in left field. Many times people poison their bodies with alcohol, drugs, tobacco, and food that are not good for the body. I heard a person give an example of how we should regard our bodies.

If someone gave you a prize race horse, you would not give the horse tobacco, drugs, or feed that are not good for his body, because the horse is valuable. There will be a price to pay for whatever we put in our bodies. There are natural laws, and if you violate them, you will pay.

Sometime we shorten our life because we do not take proper care of our body. A good friend of mine violated the natural laws of proper diet, exercise, and rest. I believe, it shortened his life by many years. Pastor Kirskey was a man who really cared about people, but he died from diabetes at age 48. I often think that had he taken care of his body, he could have lived longer and could have helped many more people. Even in his sickness he was still trying to help others. He died shortly after having both of his legs amputated.

If you jump off a 20-story building without a parachute, you will suffer serious consequences. You will be lucky to end up with just broken bones instead of dying. The power from within can either be negative or positive. However, you must continue to do what is right even when you do not want to. You may not want to exercise, but you know it is best for you, and so you must develop an attitude of not giving yourself a choice. You must say, "I must exercise." If you live in accordance with the natural laws of proper eating and proper physical care, there are many blessings awaiting you.

Chapter Six

Using Our Time Wisely

"Time is a great revealer."

Jessie Shelton

Using Our Time Wisely

My father, the late Jessie Shelton, said to me many years ago, "Time is a great revealer." Time does not lie. You might wonder whether something is true. Eventually time will reveal the real deal. My father told me to be patient, if there was something I was unsure of because time would reveal the truth. Sometimes we miss valuable time with loved ones because of misunderstandings. My father was always a good provider and taught me how to be a man. However, he had demons in his past that he had to deal with.

A couple of years before he died, I realized he did not have a problem with me, but with himself. When he retired, I thought at first it was a good thing, but it was not. I had an uncle who moved to town. He would come over to my father's house early in the morning with a "drink." He and my father would drink until evening. My father had never been sick, but the alcohol destroyed his life. A year before he died, I remember telling my father that if he kept drinking he would be dead in a year.

When you are young you always want to be right, but when you get older there are many times that you wish you were wrong. I remember carrying my father into our home before he died. My father had been a big strong man, but the gin had ravaged his body. One of the last times we talked he said he did not understand when I warned him because he had only a sixth-grade education.

When you value your time with loved ones, do not let petty things prevent you from spending time together. I remember crying and wishing I had more time to spend with my father, but it was not to be. I do believe he lives on in a sense because I named my youngest son Jessie, and my oldest son is Kenneth Jr. So now, Ken and Jessie are brothers.

One night I was riding past my friend Thurmond's home. He called out to me as I was riding by and said he needed to talk to me. I told him I would be back tomorrow because I was too busy to stop then. Thurmond died that night of a heart attack. I will never know what he wanted to tell me. We should make time for our friends. I do not believe true friends are easily found.

I can recall someone telling me something which I believed was not true. Time revealed it was true. Time should bring about a change in one's life. Some people let the years pass, and there is no growth. They have not grown in their thinking or ability to handle problems. What bothered you years ago should not continue to worry you. Many times we make a decision that something is good or bad. When we encounter a problem or situation we may say this is bad, internalize it, and get upset. I can recall a number of incidents that bothered me years ago that do not bother me today. The only difference is that I have changed my thinking concerning such matters.

As the years move on, you should desire wisdom. I might have destructive behavior as a young person, but as I mature, I should change and grow. I will never forget seeing a man collecting bottles and cans. I could see on his face what alcohol and drugs had done to him. I went to school with this man. Imagine seeing this man, who is 55 years old, pushing a shopping cart and picking up bottles and cans.

I believe everyone has a purpose. A person is not like a parasite that only takes from the land and does not give back. What do you want your legacy to be? Many are tricked into believing they can live like a hedonist who seeks only pleasure; that is not the case. I remember when I was smoking marijuana and getting high every day. I started to wonder why I was having a consistent headache. It dawned on me I was probably having headaches because of my life style. Many lives are destroyed because people believe there are no consequences to their actions.

When we are young we often feel invincible and think nothing will harm us. That is a trick from the pit of hell. How many careers have been destroyed by starting a destructive activity? From every walk of life some career has been destroyed by bad behavior. Quite often, when a person participates in bad behavior it may appear that he or she is "getting away with it" and there will be no consequences for such behavior. There are countless people who thought they were getting away with bad behavior only to discover that the trick played was on them. Consider the person who thinks he will continue drug use to the weekend. When I was out in the world, there was a saying:

"You running around with your nose snotty but you better ask somebody." What goes on in the dark eventually comes to light. There are consequences for all behavior.

When facing a situation you do not like, you should ask yourself this question: is this really that important? Many things, when we look back, we find out were not really that important. There is an old saying, "Don't make a mountain out of a mole hill." I remember missing a plane once. I thought the attendant had said one gate so I went there and sat down to wait. I saw the time the flight would leave but by the time I realized it was leaving from a different gate, the flight had left. I must admit I did not handle it very well until I changed my thinking concerning the situation.

The only way you are going to achieve success through adversity is by maintaining the right mental attitude. I was accustomed to airport gate areas only displaying flight information on flights leaving from that gate, but this was not the case this time. It was not an airline which I usually used. Well, that was the wrong gate, and a few minutes before departure I was still trying to find the right gate. I asked an attendant, but she was very rude and gave me no information. I frantically tried to find the right gate because I did not want to miss another flight. After what seemed a lifetime, I found the departure gate and got to the plane just before the door closed. I did learn from that experience to check the gate information for myself to make sure I arrived at the correct gate.

The only person you have control over is yourself. An individual can be nasty and rude, but we have no control over the person. However, every individual can have control of their

Using Our Time Wisely

own emotions and how they responds to situations. You need to be careful not to let your emotions get out of control. We live in a world of change. Events and conditions of human life are continually changing.

Many of us misuse and abuse time. Time is so ill-considered that few have proper respect for time. White or Black, rich or poor, young or old, no one can escape time. Time is no respecter of persons. You are given only so much time, so you should use it wisely. Many people fail to realize how swiftly time moves. If I ask you what time it is the time will have already changed before I finish my question.

A time account is different from a bank account. You write a certain number of checks, and at the end of the day you can do a tally and know just how much money you have left. In a time account, we use our time second by second, minute by minute, hour by hour, and day by day, etc. When our time runs out, there is no more.

You should look within yourself to give your life meaning and purpose. During difficult times you must hold on to hope and believe better days are ahead. If the current situation is not what you want, you should keep a vision of the life you want to create. Over time we realize our vision will be a self-fulfilling prophecy. The vision can be used for good or bad.

The Flying Wallendas was a high-wire act that performed 75 feet above ground. In 1978, Karl Wallenda fell off the high wire to his death. His wife said all he had talked about and thought about during the prior three months was falling.

Mrs. Wallenda said he had never before constantly talked about falling. Mr. Wallenda's loss of confidence contributed to his death even though he had many reasons to be confident. He had the wrong focus. This is the "Wallenda Factor."

During difficult times you must not throw away or abandon your confidence. You need to be confident and not give into the "Wallenda Factor." Faith continues to move forward even if the current situation seems to challenge our belief.

You need to see life with a reflective intelligence by looking at incidents in a natural way. If you see it first from within, then it will be revealed outward. The human mind is so complex and efficient that your subconscious mind will work on the goals hidden in your heart even when your conscious mind is not aware of it. Every time you choose a priority you are determining what is truly important to you, or the desire of your heart. Your heart will drift to what is most important to you.

If you are someone who prays, it does not always matter what you pray for as much as what you desire. It is possible to pray shallow, meaningless, faithless, prayers. But what your heart desires, your mind will go after. Be honest with yourself; what do you really want? Is getting high more appealing than getting delivered from drugs or alcohol? What I refer to as God, or others call the "Universe", answers prayers of believers. Do you really believe in your dream or vision?

It is important not to let your past destroy your future. Some people cannot achieve success through adversity because they keep dwelling on past events. It is important to move past your

Using Our Time Wisely

failures. Sometimes it is possible to make it through difficult times by remembering that you have already made it through in past situations. You must forgive yourself for whatever mistakes you have made in the past. Dragging the past out of the grave destroys health. When someone keeps living in the past it is like being chained to a dead body. Many people have been fatally crippled and paralyzed by carrying along something that they should have let go.

Which way is your course set — toward a bright future or looking back at past mistakes, doubt, or frustrations? Life is full of hard knocks, but it is your choice to look back at past mistakes or look forward to a brighter future.

To reach one's full potential, a person must possess courage, faith, determination, passion, and desire. To grow and contribute to life, you need to answer the following questions:

1. What stops me from achieving the following: moving forward, taking action, and being my best?
2. What determines the quality of my life?
3. Why do I do the things that I do?

You should live with confidence because of the power from within you. If you are going to be successful you cannot live by emotions, but by faith. You should allow faith to control and solve your problems.

Chapter Seven

Wisdom

Achieving Success Through Adversity

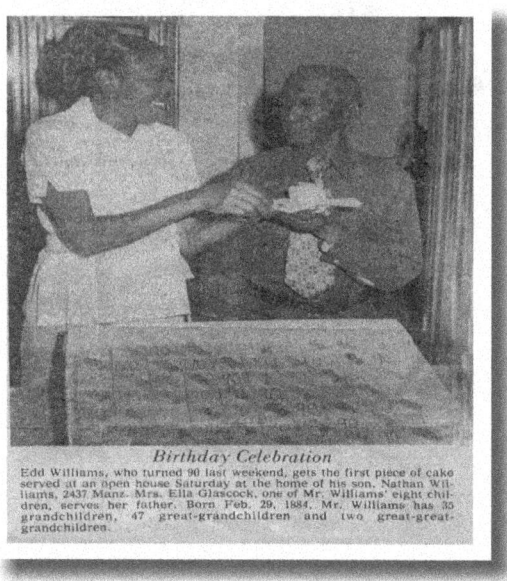

Birthday Celebration
Edd Williams, who turned 90 last weekend, gets the first piece of cake served at an open house Saturday at the home of his son, Nathan Williams, 2437 Manz. Mrs. Ella Glascock, one of Mr. Williams' eight children, serves her father. Born Feb. 29, 1884, Mr. Williams has 35 grandchildren, 47 great-grandchildren and two great-great-grandchildren.

Aunt Ella & Grandpa Ed Williams

"I'm grateful for all my problems. As each of them was overcome, I became stronger and more able to meet those yet to come. I grew on my difficulties."

J. C. Penney

WISDOM

When I was five I would walk and talk with my grandfather Ed Williams whom I called my Pa Pa. We would walk and talk about life. Pa Pa was the wisest man I ever knew. Grandpa Ed was a short and very gentle man. All the children in the neighborhood called him Grandpa, whether they were related to him or not. When my grandfather was living with us, he and I would walk from my home to East Park Manor where some of my relatives lived. As we walked, I would ask my Pa Pa many different questions about life. He always had an answer, and I thought he was very smart. I was discussing this with my mother who at first said smartest, but when I gave my opinion, she said wisest was more accurate. My Pa Pa demonstrated honesty and integrity.

One beautiful summer day we were out walking, and we stopped by a store. My grandfather wanted to purchase an item on credit, and the lady pulled out a piece of paper and Pa Pa signed with an "X". I was startled, I had expected him to sign his name. I was about five years old, and I could sign my name.

I asked him as we began to walk out of the store, "Pa Pa, that's how you sign your name?" He answered, "Yes." He was not embarrassed. My grandfather continued by telling me he could count his money so no one could cheat him.

When discussing this with my mother, she said he could get anything he wanted all over town on credit. That included clothing, furniture, groceries, etc. just by signing an "X". What can anyone purchase today by just signing an "X"? Today they have to check with the credit bureau to make sure you are a good credit risk.

I so enjoyed walking and talking with Pa Pa about life. I began to understand that not all education comes from a book. It is valuable to develop relationships and learn from our elders. It is important that you tell your loved ones that you love them. I was not going to write about this because, to be honest, I have found it hard to say I love you. I have tried to show my love by actions, but I know a person needs to hear that you love him or her. It hurts me to write this, but it is the truth.

When Pa Pa was diagnosed with stomach cancer and was on his death bed at the age of 93, he sent for me because he wanted to talk to me. I had uncles that were much older, but he wanted to talk to me. When I was 5 years old and he was 75, I had looked for every chance to talk with him, and now my Pa Pa was on his death bed and he wanted to talk to me. I walked into his bedroom at my Aunt Tennie's house, and he was lying in the bed. We talked about life and death. I laid my head on the bed and said, "Pa Pa, I love you and I do not want you to die." My grandfather's eyes opened, and he said, "Kenny Ray, that is the first time you ever said that to me."

I cannot express enough the fact that your nervous system does not truly know the difference between what you imagine in great detail and what you are actually experiencing. I sit here 35 years later, and this is not easy. I remember falling down on my knees, crying when I heard that my Pa Pa had a short time to live. The tears fell like a waterfall. I felt God ask me a question in my spirit, "Would I rather for my Pa Pa to stay in pain or to be relieved of his suffering?" I loved my Pa Pa too much and did not want him to continue to suffer. It was selfish for me to want him to live in the pain he was experiencing.

The Bible says "go to the ant thou sluggard, consider her ways, and be wise: having no chief, overseer, or ruler, the ant nevertheless provides her bread in the summer, and gathers her food in the harvest." Nature can take the smallest creature of creation to teach us a lesson. As we go about our lives, we overlook powerful lessons to be learned from God's creations. It would be good for us to examine the habits of ants and see what we can learn from them. See what they do, and how they do it, and learn all we can.

The ant is among the smallest insects on earth. They build colonies (cities) under the earth. They have survived from the beginning of time by doing something that comes to them by instinct from God. Ants establish well defined trails between water, food, and the nest. Have you ever seen a lazy ant? They can carry 100 times their weight. It is comparable to a person who weighs 100 pounds carrying 10,000 pounds. You cannot be lazy and realize your dreams.

If you want to achieve your goal or realize your dreams, you must be willing to work. It will not just fall in your lap. It will take hard work to realize your dream. Even with God - given talent it still takes work to reach our full potential. Ants show great discipline in building their cities. You need to be disciplined. James 1:5 says, "If any of you lack wisdom, he should ask of God, who gives generously to all without finding fault, and it will be given to him. But when he asks, he must believe and not doubt, because he who doubts is like a wave of the sea, blown and tossed by the wind." Wisdom does not always come because the years pass.

As the saying goes, "There's no fool like an old fool." If you are going to be wise at different stages of your life, you should handle situations in an effective way. If you are a wise person, you should handle things different at 35 than you did at 19 years old. Each person will have different stages in their life. It is important how you handle each phase. As you get older, there are some adjustments you will need to make because of unexpected situations. No one can improve his situation unless he can improve himself.

You should also seek wise counsel. Hank Aaron of the baseball Hall Of Fame made a wise statement: "Be careful before you make choices. Avoid shortcuts. They are quick fixes and unrewarding." That is a true statement.

When I got out of the military, I enrolled in a two-year college. I took a Political Science class and I was flunking. I did not realize everyone in the class knew I was flunking. I did not show anyone my papers. However, they found out some way. One day the instructor stated that slavery was not that bad. I immediately began to debate him on the issue. Anyone who understood slavery would have to agree it was very bad for many, especially when you consider that slaves had no rights and could be sold or killed. Your loved ones could be sold and you would never see them again. Basically a slave had no rights. I was shocked to hear an instructor make that statement.

After I got through debating the instructor on slavery, a man of Indian descent came to me and offered to help me understand how to pass the class. After he heard me debate the instructor, he realized that I did not have a learning disability. I was under the impression I could read something one time and be ready to take the test. But for many it requires rote learning. After he showed me how to study, I ended up finishing the class with a "C". It was a turning point for me in college, because I went on to get my liberal arts degree and later my Bachelors Degree in Public Administration.

It is important to appreciate good friends or acquaintances because not everyone will have your best interest at heart. Many years passed before I obtained, at the urging of my board of directors, my Bachelors Degree in Public Administration. I would get the requisite education to get the job I wanted. I would wonder why I needed additional education because I was already doing the job. However, when I was hired as Executive Director of Muskegon-Oceana Community Action Partnership, the board of directors made a condition of employment that I get my Bachelor's Degree.

First, I talked with some employees at the college, and they could not or would not get all the information about my previous credits from Grand Valley State University. However, I was able to get in touch with Dr. Myron Mast, and he performed a valuable service by searching the records. He saved me about two years of study and a lot of money to get my degree. Just think, if I had been a nasty or rude person, do you think he would have made that extra effort? He most certainly would not have put forth any real effort. You treat everyone as well as you can, not because you want something but because it is the right thing to do. Sometimes you will receive benefits you never expected. It is also important to emphasize that not everyone can give good advice. Some people will tell you to do things that they would not do themselves.

I have found that counsel may seem wiser after I have gone through an experience. This does not mean you have to experience everything to learn. I do not have to take heroin to know it will destroy my life. I can just observe other people who have walked down that road. You may think one way by looking from the sidelines, but when you get in the game, after receiving a few bumps and bruises, you may be kinder and more thoughtful in your advice. Not that everyone wants good advice, because some people love misery, no matter what you say to them. As the old saying goes, "The difference between the wise man and the fool is that the wise person learns from his mistakes and the fool keeps making the same mistake."

Wisdom tells us that whatever storm we face at this moment, that storm will not last forever. You can look at the elements and see no matter how bad the storm seems to be, there comes a day when the sun does shine again. You must continue to press forward no matter how you feel. If you are going to achieve success you cannot let negative emotions hinder your progress.

It is said that the eagle is a bird that will fly into the storm and let the wind of the storm take it to new heights. You need to allow the storm to take you to a new height. Without the winds of storms you cannot become the person you need to be. Most people do not enjoy storms, but to be honest we do not evolve into the best person possible without the storms and disappointments of life.

Even when people do not understand you it is important that you stand for what you know is right until something shows that you are wrong. I saw something interesting on a flight home from a conference in Los Angeles. Looking out the window, I noticed the words "no step" on the airplane wing. If you are going to live a wise life, there are some situations or places where you should not step, physically or mentally. If you walk into some situations, you can receive great harm. What mine fields are you walking through in your mind? There are places in your mind you should not step into, such as doubt, fear, hate, etc. Your thoughts should keep love and forgiveness in mind. I am not suggesting that it will always be easy. Nevertheless, it is what you should strive to do.

If you want to live a life of wisdom, you need to have a clear vision. Webster defines wisdom as: "1. unusual foresight' 2. a mental image produced by the imagination; Vision is to faith, what belief is to attitude." Both the hummingbird and the vulture fly over the desert. All the vulture sees is rotting meat because that is what it looks for. They thrive on that diet. Hummingbirds ignore the smelly flesh of dead animals. Instead, they look for the colorful flowers of desert plants. The vultures live on what was. They live in the past. They fill themselves with what is dead and no longer alive, whereas the hummingbirds live on what is alive; they seek new life. They fill themselves with the freshness of life.

Each bird finds what it is looking for and so do we. Take a closer look at the vulture as a metaphor. Some people only see what is bad and never what is good! And some cannot break away from the past — past hurts and disappointments. The hummingbirds live on new life. Do you keep a picture in your mind of a brighter future? If you can hold this picture in your mind and are willing to pay your dues, it can become a reality.

Life is a journey and every journey has a destination. Everyone ends up somewhere in life. A clear vision with courage to follow through dramatically increases your chance of coming to the end of your life with deep satisfaction and a sense of accomplishment. "I did it! I succeeded! I finished well. My life counted!" Unless you discover your divine mission, you will never reach your full potential. I think the following story will bring home the point.

In 1212, Stephen, a French shepherd boy, claimed he had a divine vision. He was instructed to take a letter to the King of France. More than 30 thousand children followed him, but instead their voyage landed some of them in the bottom of the sea because two of the ships were said to have sunk without any survivors. The others were said to have been sold into slavery in North Africa. Two slave traders, Hugo Ferreus ("Iron Hugo") and William Porcus ("William the Pig"), tricked the travelers into thinking they believed them and promised to take the travelers to their requested destination in France for free. The pair instead sold them into slavery. The children were following someone else's vision, not their own.

A vision is born in the soul of a man or woman who is consumed with the tension between what is and what could be.

A true vision is more than simply what could be. What could be is simply an idea or dream but vision also implies conviction. It is not only what can be done but something that must be done. It is something that must happen. It moves you from passive concern to action. Conviction is what gives a sense of urgency. To be wise you must follow your vision rather than someone else's vision.

Chapter Eight

Enjoy the Journey

"Success is to be measured not so much by the position one has reached in life, as by the obstacles which one has overcome while trying to succeed."

Booker T. Washington

Enjoy the Journey

We need to enjoy the journey. So often we keep waiting for some time in the future to bring us happiness rather than enjoying the moment. We travel through life thinking that when we purchase something, or have special relationship, or take a certain trip we will find real happiness. We need to enjoy the moment because none of us knows how long we will be here. If you were told you had six months to live, there are many things that you may think are important today that would not be significant or would not be worth getting upset about.

I must be honest! I had a wakeup call writing this chapter. It is possible to state a great truth and not totally live by that truth yourself. The statement is true. I do enjoy the journey most of the time, but for awhile I had wondered when God would give me the big breakthrough I am anticipating rather than totally enjoying this time in my life.

I was told a friend I have known since childhood had a serious illness, pancreatic cancer. Very few people diagnosed with this disease survive for very long. I had to be honest with myself and ask the question put forward by the title of this chapter, "Enjoying the Journey." Am I enjoying the journey as I should? I am glad to say that my friend Bishop Willie Burrel is doing well and consented to the following interview:

Ken: Bishop, I want to thank-you for taking the time to give me this interview.

Bishop Burrel: Reverend Dr. Ken, I was glad to give this interview for your book.

Ken: As I mentioned, the title of the book is Achieving Success Through Adversity. I had been so stressed I lost sight of reality. I was working with some preachers who had promised me a job, but they did not follow through. I was diagnosed as paranoid schizophrenic. I was very hurt, but it was a defining moment. It turned out to be a blessing because I deal with my problems totally different now. All of us will have a defining moment.

Bishop: That is true.

Ken: The one thing that seems to be crushing at one point can later in life turn out to be a blessing.

Bishop: A preacher I had delivered an excellent sermon entitled, "Set Up For A Miracle." At my church she talked about how God sets us up, and we have to go through something to receive God's blessing because this is part of the process. Adversity leads to a breakthrough if we stay the course. In the sermon she used the example of a man who had been at the pool of Bethesda for thirty-eight years and before his healing he made a lot of excuses as many people do. God already knows what we are going through.

Ken: I think that the key is not to be discouraged.

Bishop: I went through my time of — I won't say doubt — but a time of great concern when they told me I have this illness that normally kills people.

Ken: So you were diagnosed with pancreatic cancer?

Bishop: Yes, the doctor told me straight out that even with treatment most people do not live a year. I asked the doctor if they could operate and he told me I would probably die on the table. The cancer had spread to my liver and other parts of my body.

Ken: What was your first reaction?

Bishop: As I mentioned earlier, I was concerned, but I know God is able. Even if He does not heal me, I still know he is able to perform a miracle. I found out while going to a council meeting. I was driving and had a lapse for a moment and then a semi-truck pulled out in front of me. [His wife calls the Bishop. Honey, I am having lunch with Revd. Dr. Ken. I will call you back after lunch.] My wife told me to tell you hello.

Ken: Okay.

Bishop: My mother and I were going to a church conference in Flint Michigan and I hit that truck going 75 miles an hour. The accident nearly totaled the car. It seemed like my mother and I were not hurt at all. The Lord protected us because the car went down into the ravine and flipped over. Some days later, I started feeling a tremendous amount of pain. It was like someone took a stake and stuck it though my back. I went to the doctor and had an x-ray and a doctor's examination showed no problem. My blood pressure went up, and I lost my appetite. I was weighing about 234 pounds, and I lost 50 pounds. I had wanted to lose weight but not like that. I could not eat. An endoscopic biopsy in Grand Rapids revealed that the cancer covered 85 percent of my pancreas. It also surrounded my siliac artery which made surgery all but impossible. I asked the doctor how long do people normally live? He said one of his patients lived two weeks after the diagnosis. He said that was the only good news he could give me. The last person had lived just two weeks!

Ken: What did you say after that?

Bishop: Well, Ken, I felt God had more purpose for my life than to let me die and go out like that. I was in so much pain. I went to Houston, Texas, and they said my condition was so severe they did not know if they could treat me. I told my staff about my condition. We decided on the University of Michigan Hospital in Ann Arbor where they gave me a special treatment. My wife, Zandra, is a jewel. The person who helped me the most during my illness was my wife. She went on the Internet and learned about the body's acid versus alkaline. She has just been a jewel. I drink a lot of juice now. We purchased a very good juicer and we eat a lot of organic foods.

Ken: So one of the things that helped you is that you felt you had not fulfilled the purpose God had for you?

Bishop: The people of God really helped by calling and

giving words of encouragement. You need people who will speak positive. You don't need to hear anything negative.

Ken: Do you look at life differently?

Bishop: Yes, you appreciate things a lot like driving your car and, in my case, having my hair back. The people of God and my family. And I thank God for being who He is. I read Scriptures and quoted the word of God.

Ken: When someone is going through a crisis what are some things they need to keep in mind?

Bishop: Stay focused on what the word of God says. Isaiah 53:4: "But He was wounded for our transgressions, he was bruised for our iniquities; the chastisement of our peace was upon him; and with his stripes we are healed; I shall live and not die." It is important to keep in mind what the word of God says.

Ken: The accident turned out to be a blessing.

Bishop: The accident turned out to be a blessing. It was a blessing in disguise. Because of it the cancer was diagnosed. It might not have been found until it was too late. God works in mysterious ways. There were times I was so sick from treatments, from chemo, I had to be hospitalized and could not eat.

Ken: Through all the sickness how did you keep going? How did you process it? Did you stay encouraged?

Bishop: Ken, you know through all my sickness I only missed two Sundays of church. Ken, through all my sickness I continued to believe I was going to get better. I remember when I was in the hospital at the University of Michigan there was a basketball court I could see outside my window. I would say to myself one day I am going to get back on the basketball court and play basketball. I was to go to a national meeting, and I took my wife and mother on vacation to Miami. And then gradually my pain started to go away. The tumor started to shrink. My wife was a real jewel. She gradually stopped giving me the pain medication. I did not realize she had stopped. My brother was an excellent help as assistant pastor. You must have something inside to keep going. You must never give up.

Ken: Do you have any additional comments?

Bishop: No, but I would like a copy of your book when you are done because that is a good title.

Ken: I will make sure you get a copy.

As I think back on my conversation with Bishop Burrel, he always kept an encouraged spirit through all that he endured. No matter how bad the situation got he always believed that his situation would get better. I think about what the doctor told him, that the last patient had lived only two weeks. That took a tremendous leap of faith to believe that God would deliver him through such a devastating situation. Bishop Burrel did not push the panic button. He was able to keep his composure. If we are going to make it through a crisis, we must hold on to our composure. Our God, or a Higher Power, is able to do everything but fail.

If you find yourself in a difficult situation, no matter how it is for someone else, your situation can come out better. It took a tremendous amount of faith for Bishop Burrel to keep going when the only good news the doctor could give him was that the last person diagnosed with pancreatic cancer died in two weeks. Many people would have been completely done in. Their thoughts would have shifted to the impossibility of survival because the last person only lived two weeks. No matter how dark it gets you must hold on to your faith if you are going to achieve success through adversity.

You need to focus on things that are really important. Let us not take the people who love us for granted. It is not a daily occurrence to encounter people that really love us. No one knows the day or hour he or she will leave here. So you must ask yourself what is really important. I believe very few people reach the end of their lives and wish they had made more millions. Most probably would say I wish I had spent more time with family and friends or just enjoyed life. I believe all or most would say that riches are not very important.

If we are going to enjoy the journey we cannot be dependent on other people to make or keep us happy. If you are going to find happiness or joy, it must come from within yourself. You cannot depend on others to give you happiness. Because there will be those moments when you wish so dearly someone understands, and it will seem like no one does understand or care. Sometimes people are so busy living their lives and dealing with their problems, they do not have time to think about your situation. For me personally the only real joy comes in my relationship with God.

If you are going to have real joy there are some things you need to keep in mind. 1. Some people may be with you one day and gone the next. 2. Material possessions — you can buy a diamond and after awhile the diamond does not shine like it used to. 3. Worry only breaks your body down. When you worry, your nervous system cannot function properly so you become sick. For example, if you took your hand and closed it very tightly and then opened it, you will find vessels that are temporary broken. When you worry, circulation in your system is broken in the same way and then you become sick with different types of illnesses. Stress is one of the biggest hindrances to achieving success through adversity.

One of the biggest problems people have in dealing with stress is worrying about tomorrow instead of being content with the burden of the current day. Most of the things we worry about will never happen. More people are killed by worry than are killed by work. It is said an ounce of prevention is worth more than a pound of cure. The key is to work to prevent certain ailments. Most people are capable of doing great work if they do not get in the habit of worrying about it. If stress is not handled properly it can affect every part of your body, eg., headaches, strokes, heart attacks, nervous breakdowns, etc. Stress is something that saps us of our energy and distracts from our goals.

All stress can't be totally avoided. Stress must be recognized, confronted, and managed. That is the only way it can be transformed into positive energy. It can be used to stimulate and inspire us. Stress helps us achieve higher goals. If you are going to handle stress it is important to have the right information. A person must understand the effects of stress on his or her body and mind. You must learn to identify its cause and prepare a workable program of stress reduction. There are many relaxation exercises to reduce stress.

You need to learn to change what you can and accept what you cannot change. This should call to mind The Serinity Prayer: "God grant me the serenity to accept the things I cannot change; courage to change the things I can; and wisdom to know the difference between the two." A few things you should remember:

1. We cannot totally eliminate all stress from our lives.

2. If stress is managed properly it can be a good thing to help you achieve your goal.

3. Stress is a killer if not handled properly.

4. When you are in a stressful situation you need to shift your thinking by reading or listening to something positive: turn to music, a relaxation CD, or exercise.

And finally, if you let each day take care of itself you will find peace and happiness.

Chapter Nine

Keys to Success

"Do the things you fear and the death of fear is certain."

Ralph Waldo Emerson

Keys to Success

Success leaves footprints. If you live in an area where it snows and someone walks a path before you do, he leaves his footprints in the snow. There are things successful people do. If you emulate what successful people have done, you will have success. I do not mean trying to be someone else. Everyone has a purpose for his or her life. As the title of this chapter states, there are "Keys to Success," but you must have the right keys. Not just any key will open the door to your home or start your car. There have been times I have thrown keys away because after a period of time I did not know what the keys unlock. You must have the right key and the right type of plan. Not just any plan will work. Just going through the motions without a good blueprint is wasting time. A person can sit in a rocking chair and move a great deal, but he is not going to accomplish very much.

When I discuss how successful people live their lives, I mean that successful people are honest with themselves. They have a definite plan for their lives. They work to master a skill. You can acquire a good life by mastering a skill or indulging your passion. A person needs to find his or her specific purpose in life. A person can be successful at one point in life and not be successful at another time of his life, or a person can be a failure at one time and a success later when he changes his pattern of thinking and behavior. You must determine what you really want out of life and what you are willing to give.

Sometimes you feel distant from a situation and are not keen to relate to it or explain it. I want to stress how important it is to have the right mindset. Your prospects will be determined by how you think. What happens is not as important as what happens within you. You can feel sorry for yourself, but it is not going to help your situation. You need to develop a plan that will change your situation and believe the plan will work. You also need to be thankful even if you are unemployed.

I was once an executive. I thought it embarrassing to stand in the unemployment line. I would look around and think of previous difficult times. I remembered being unemployed years ago and thinking how I really did not want to be there. I overlooked the fact that unemployment checks were helping me pay the bills. When I received a letter indicating I would not receive any more checks some weeks later, I started wishing I could get back in that line. Even in difficult times we should all have a spirit of gratitude. You must focus on what you want rather than what you do not want. It is possible to become so preoccupied by a problem that we do not think about a solution.

The nervous system is like an electrical wire. If you break the wire, it cannot turn on the electrical appliance. When you worry, it is similar to breaking an electrical circuit. Everyone has issues to deal with, but the key is "how" we deal with them. Many entertainers are wealthy, but they are not necessarily happy. Many are even strung out on drugs. Many people try to fill a void in their lives. I believe there is a place within us that is reserved for a Higher Power, and no matter what you to try to fill that void with — drugs, sex, money — it can only be healed by a connection with a Higher Power or, according to my belief, Jesus Christ. I am trying to write something that many people can relate to, but I feel I would be dishonest if I did not at least express my belief. I do realize that everyone who reads this book may not have the same beliefs. However, there is a map we can use that can help us deal with the adversities of life. If there were no bad times, how would we really enjoy the good times?

Some years ago, a union was formed at the agency. The workers were told how unfair they were being treated because some people within the agency were making considerably more money. I often thought they really did not know how well off they were because they were working. However, the comparison was not fair because one group was college educated, and the other had high school diplomas. Many of the complaining workers had never worked before. They thought they were in a bad situation, whereas it was rather good. However, they had nothing to compare their job situation with. They had full medical benefits and a good salary. They had the summer off and could draw unemployment compensation. They could do whatever they wanted during the summer, and they still had some income. When the agency lost that program, another agency took over. Many of the same people were not hired because they lacked the requisite education. The few who were hired did not have the summer off with pay. When the people who thought things were bad saw an alternative situation, they no longer had a job. They did not realize how well off they had been. You may think your situation is bad, but it could be worse.

You need to look around and think about the things you can be thankful for. What about the times when you do not feel like getting out of bed? What do you think is going to determine the course of your life? There is the battle of the mind. If we lose this battle, there is no hope. Some battles you might not fight well, but the most important thing is not to lose the war. You cannot let others' negative comments break your spirit.

I once watched a dance contest on television. One judge kept criticizing one person but passing him on. He would say that the dancer had let his partner down but that he was going to pass him on. The dancers performed different styles of dance. When the performers were not performing the type of dance they normally do, they did not do it as well. The audience gave the performer a thunderous applause, but two judges gave him nothing but criticism. The audience started to boo the judges, but the performer stopped them, and said the judges were right. Dancers need to study. The dancer believed that God had him there for a purpose. Because he had the right attitude, Debbie Allen gave him a scholarship to her dance school. If we are going to get the results we want, we must have the right attitude. If your thinking is wrong, you cannot get the right result.

There is nothing more important than how you think. Even if we believe something is false, it still can have a devastating effect on our health. I read in Dr. Herbert Benson's book "Timeless Healing - The Power and Biology of Belief", a story of a country where there was a belief that young Aborigine people should not eat hens. One of the young Aborigine men went off to college. Upon his return home, his uncle asked him was he now eating hen. The young man said of course not because it was forbidden. His uncle said, "Remember when you were young? I tricked you into eating hen." Within twenty-four hours, the young man was dead. The hen had not been poisonous, but the young man believed in the taboo. That belief was powerful enough to end his life within hours. The nervous system accepted it as fact even though it was wrong. You must press on and continue to do what you know to be right.

Your life should not be dictated by your emotions because there may be times when you are not inclined to do what may be necessary. I believe you have to experience some circumstances to understand, relate, and have empathy for others. You must have the right conversation with yourself. You may not be comfortable with your situation, but you have to decide what situation you hope to create. To become successful, you must make up your mind to get up regardless of how many times you get knocked down. Do not let someone else determine what success should be for you.

I was watching an "Encore" reenactment of a poor young man who was a caddy. He wanted to be a professional golfer. His father said it was not something he should aspire to. They were poor and should stay in their place. Many of the rich people he worked for were rude to him, but he kept trying. The first time he tried, he was not successful. Eventually, he did get an opportunity to play as an amateur in the U. S. Open and won twice. He became a successful business man and an ambassador. The poor young caddy became a multimillionaire. If we want to achieve our dreams, we must realize that we will have to handle disappointment and defeat before we succeed.

This story reminds us that it is important with whom you associate and spend time. You should not spend much time with someone who is always negative because it will affect you. To be successful, you must decide what you really want and what you plan to give in exchange. If you hope to be happy, you must decide what you want to become and attain. You will never be happy if you let someone else decide for you. I heard Earl Nightingale give a good description of success: "Success is to be determined by what you determine is a worthy goal." Success is not getting what someone else has, or, as we commonly say, keeping up with the Joneses. If someone buys a new car, we feel that we must go out and buy one, or you do something to make someone else happy. These are not the components of success. You have to set your own goal and then do all you can to realize it.

You must find out what you love doing. That is your passion. When you find out what you love to do, your work is a labor of love. It is self-motivating. You must find something that excites you or creates a burning desire in you. To achieve your goal, you have to develop good habits. If you do not acquire good habits, bad habits will destroy you. It is important to hold on to hope. Romans 4:18 says, "Who in hope believed against hope to the end that he might become a father of many nations, according to that which had been spoken, so shall thy seed be." It seems to be a contradiction, but what the text is saying is that no matter how dark it may seem we need to hold on to hope.

It is important to take proper actions. If a person wants to fulfill his destiny, he must be willing to do, not just talk. Any recurring emotion will move from the conscious to the subconscious mind. You will get hunches and ideas on what to do. It is important that you use your mind. That is the only thing that separates us from any other creature on earth.

Keys to Success

Madam C. J. Walker, was born Sarah Breedlove. She became a pioneer in the modern cosmetics industry. Ms. Walker is a good example of a person who used her mind. Born the daughter of freed slaves in 1867, she built a successful cosmetics company and became one of the most influential African American women of the late 19th and early 20th centuries. Working as a laundry woman, she managed to save enough money to educate her daughter. During the 1890's Madam Walker began to suffer from a scalp ailment that caused her to lose hair. Embarrassed by her appearance, she experimented with a variety of home-made remedies and products made by another woman entrepreneur, Annie Malone.

In 1905, Madam Walker became a sales agent for Malone and moved to Denver where she married Charles Joseph Walker. At the Thirteenth Annual Convention of the National Negro Business League in 1912, no women were included on the schedule of speakers. Madam Walker shocked the participants when she walked up and claimed the podium from moderator Booker T. Washington: "Surely you are not going to shut the door in my face. I am in a business that is a credit to the womanhood of our race. I am a woman who started in business seven years ago with only $1.50. This year, up to the 19th day of this month, I have taken in $18,000. [Prolonged applause] This makes a grand total of $63,049, made in my hair business in Indianapolis." [Applause]

Eventually Walker's products were the basis of a thriving national corporation employing over 3,000 people at one point. Madam Walker's aggressive marketing strategy combined with relentless ambition led her to be recognized as the first self-made African-American woman millionaire. Madam Walker shows what a person can do with a burning desire.

If your inner world is positive, your outer world will show improvement.

Information on Madam C. J. Walker was cited at the following websites: (www.aboutInventors.com)(www.nps.gov/history).

Chapter Ten

You Must Have the Right Picture

"Whether you believe you can do a thing or you can't you are right."

Henry Ford

You Must Have the Right Picture

If you do not have the situation that you want, you must visualize a better one in your mind. You must see your situation getting better. It does not matter what situation you are in, what matters is the situation you have created in your mind. "You cannot consistently perform in a manner which is inconsistent with the way you see yourself," states Dr. Joyce Brothers. How do you see yourself? It is less important how others see you than how you see yourself.

We need to remember that adversity can be a positive thing although it may not seem so when we are going through a bad situation. Adversity is what defines us. It is easy to have a great attitude and a positive outlook when things are going our way. The question is how do we withstand tough times. Consider this fact. Walt Disney experienced bankruptcy and a nervous breakdown but still made it to the top.

We must push through the adversity we face. If we do not,

we would not be prepared for winning. People are successful because they face adversity head on and thereby gain strength and skill. They do not take the easy path and avoid resistance. Adversity is a powerful teacher.

One person who showed the value of adversity is Helen Keller, who was handicapped at birth. She was not able to speak, hear, or see during her long life. Nevertheless, she became a famous author and worldwide celebrity because of her charm and wisdom. One of her quotes I like very much is "The worst thing is not to be without sight but not to have a vision."

When you get discouraged and cannot seem to make it, there is one dynamic you cannot do without. It is worth more than rubies and diamonds. That dynamic is relentless effort. You must never give up! Success cannot be achieved without hard work and consistent effort.

The bamboo tree grows very little the first four years, and then in the fifth year it grows 80–90 feet tall. The bamboo tree devotes most of its energy in the initial years to develop the rhizome system, or its roots. You cannot short cut the time it takes to establish your own rhizome system. If a person is going to be successful, he needs a system or blueprint. It is important to realize that much of the growth at the beginning is underground, just as a person's development might not be noticeable to everyone.

Have you heard of a person called an overnight success? Many times the person has been laboring for years, but it seemed no one noticed. Then after years of faithfulness to his or her

You Must Have the Right Picture

goal, the person realizes his or her dream. As you cannot rush the development of the bamboo tree, so too an individual needs to develop to be ready when the opportunity comes. You do not have to be great to start, but to become great, you must start.

You should have appropriate morals, values, and attitude. Your attitude will determine your altitude in life. If you do not have the right morals or values it may cause you to live a life of guilt. If you live a life of guilt, you cannot focus on your goals. You need a clear conscience about the life you are living. If you can change the picture in your mind, you can change your life. That is why it is important that you not tell everyone your hopes and dreams because some people will plant seeds of doubt. They may not say it, but their looks may say they do not really believe you can accomplish your dream. It would not have been planted in you if was not for you to achieve. You need to have the inner strength to pursue your goal. The current situation may not be to your liking, but you must hold on to the vision of a better day.

You should also bring humor and laughter into your life. Use books, CD's and movies. Laughter is important in a person's life. You must be careful in your thinking. Visualize a better life or relationship. Your imagination is the preview of coming events. Is your dominant thought fear or success? You create your world through your thought pattern. If you want a good picture, you must focus your camera on the subject you want to capture. To keep focused on the right picture, you must also consider your health.

To live a successful life discipline is vital. Whatever you eat or drink should be done in moderation. Many people overindulge and suffer health problems. Walking three times a week for 30 minutes is very helpful. Too many people just sit idly without getting necessary exercise. More people in the United States die from cardiovascular disease than from any other cause. It used to be considered a disease of men, but it is now a leading killer of women. In 2004 (the most recent year for which statistics are available), cardiovascular disease claimed the lives of 410, 365 men and 461,152 women. For women, that equals more than the next five leading causes of death combined: cancer, emphysema, Alzheimer's disease, diabetes, and accidents. (Special Report 2008, Cleveland Clinic and the Heart Advisor)

Two diet plans that I have found helpful are the South Beach diet and DASH. You can go to Google and type in DASH for more information. A healthy life style should not be based on a temporary plan but a permanent way of living. If you take control of your diet and exercise, you can live a healthy life.

If there is a goal you want to achieve, you must be focused. It should be crystal clear that to get out of adversity you need to develop a plan. You need a definite plan, and if that plan does not work, you need to look for a new plan. However, you need to make sure you have given the plan enough time to work. Some people attain great success by holding on to their plan or dream even though other people said it was not possible. You must not keep looking back at the past. You must get a firm conviction in your mind that you can do anything you really want to do. You must reaffirm that you have the power to overcome this adversity. You must remember that trials make us better.

You should never forget it is not what happens around you but what happens within you that matters. You must believe things eventually will get better. You must remember when tested that

You Must Have the Right Picture

when you pass there is a great reward waiting for you. I cannot emphasize enough the importance of faith. I read an article many years ago about a sheriff and his faith. An escaped convict had managed to get the sheriff's gun. The Sheriff expected the escapee to kill since he had taken his gun. The sheriff says to the convict, "I know you are going to kill me so let me get on my knees and make peace with my maker." The convict did not shoot the sheriff. The convict said the reason he did not kill the sheriff was because the sheriff demonstrated tremendous faith. You must hold on to your faith if you are going to make it through a midnight situation. What you listen to is important because faith comes from what we hear.

You must not let your spirit be broken, because if your spirit is broken there is no hope. Do not be like pike fish. Some pike fish were placed in an aquarium with minnows. For a time the pike fish were devouring the minnows until a glass partition was placed between the pike fish and the minnows. The pike fish kept hitting the glass partition and became discouraged. The glass partition was then lifted. Because the pike fish had had so many disappointments, the minnows could just swim by the pike fish and they would not even try to eat the minnows. Please do not be like those pike fish because you may have had some disappointments so you quit trying. On the other side of the glass partition there is victory.

A successful person expects to win. Do not pursue your goal half way. Give it all you have. There are a few questions you need to answer in pursuit of your goal. What is your passion? What do you love to do? What would you do even if you did not get paid? What comes easily to you but hard to others? Any goal you desire to achieve should not violate the law of God or the Universe. Begin to act as if the dream has already been accomplished. You must act in every way as the person you wish to become, and you will become that person. You need to steer clear of envy, anger, hate, revenge, greed, and fear because negative emotions can never produce positive results. Nothing is impossible if you truly believe. The person who has control over your attitude is you. Keep your mind focused on what you want instead of what you do not want. You must be willing to do more than what you are getting paid for.

Remember:

1. You must decide what you really want rather than several different things if you hope to achieve your dream. What am I committed to achieving? Many times people say they want to accomplish a particular objective but do not want to put in the time and effort to make it happen.

2. It is important to understand why you have decided to go after a certain goal. You need to have a compelling reason that will keep you determined to accomplish the dream during difficult times. This task is not just a day dream. If you have a compelling reason to pursue a dream, and you fail initially, you will stay determined and focused.

3. "If you can conceive and believe, you can achieve." You should constantly hold a vision of what you want to become and it will become a reality. Dorothy Brande, in her book Wake Up and Live, states that we should act as if it were impossible for us to fail. When we have that type of attitude we will go all out. Because if we start thinking it is only a possibility, we could fail. We will not make a focused effort.

4. You should not let others determine your destiny in life. It is very unusual for another person to envision you achieving your ultimate goal.

5. Those who are successful know what they want and are definite in their purpose.

6. A person who has decided what is important to him also knows what he plans to give to accomplish his objective.

7. A person who intends to achieve his goal considers the specific actions he must take to achieve it.

A good idea is a vision board. Look through magazines and get pictures of things you want, places you want to go, and, maybe, health changes you would like to make. Everyone has a vision that is either positive or negative. Our vision is a self-fulfilling prophecy. If a person is successful, he had to expect to win. Do not go after any goal half way, give it all that you have. You must continue to hold the picture of what you want to accomplish. You need to have bounce-back power.

When I was a child I loved to play with a rubber ball. No matter how hard I threw the ball down, it would bounce back. When life throws you down, you must bounce back. I remember one day taking a rubber ball apart to see what was inside, to find out why it was able to bounce back. I found it was the composition of the ball itself. What kind of internal strength do you have? Because your ability to bounce back will be determined by your inner strength. Success takes time, so do not lose heart. Just press toward your goal. Follow the "Bounce Back Theory." I guarantee you will win in life!

Author Biography

Kenneth R. Shelton, Sr. is a very dynamic speaker and he possess many years of experience in the public speaking arena. Ken has always cultivated lasting relationships by demonstrating his capability to effectively communicate with diverse audiences in many geographical areas. He is currently the Executive Director and CEO of Muskegon – Oceana Community Action Partnership, Inc., an anti - poverty agency in Western Michigan.

Because of the hardships that Ken has experienced and had to overcome in his life, he can present a message that will tug on the heart stings of all those who receive it. Through knowledge that he gained in his early twenties, Ken has created an inspirational workshop entitled "Achieving Success Through Adversity." He recognizes that anyone with the right information can navigate through difficult times. Ken will share with you how to develop a success plan for your life. His message will inspire you to pursue greatness in every aspect of life. He recognizes that the ability is already in you and he will help to propel you to your highest potential. Through his many years in the Human Service industry, Ken has gained a vast knowledge of assisting individuals who are facing insurmountable odds and those who feel they are in hopeless situations.

Author Biography

Ken has well – rounded experience and knowledge of business and corporate structure. He knows what it takes to be set apart and achieve. He has skillfully gained this knowledge through the management, executive and leadership positions he has held throughout his career.

It is noteworthy to mention that individuals who have experienced Ken Shelton's message have been transformed. Transformation results include:

* Positive and improved thought processes
* Revived physical and mental state of being
* Increased understanding and sense of self – awareness
* Newfound hope and energy

Ken is well received and respected for his work in the community. He has received two Muskegon Hoodie Awards: in 2005 his agency won the *"Best Non-Profit"* award and in 2006, Ken won the *"Community Person of the Year"* award. The Hoodie awards are for the best in the community (neighborhood) and annual awardees are determined by nominations and votes from community residents.

J. RILEY

SELECTED QUOTATIONS

The gem cannot be polished without friction, nor man perfected without trials.
Chinese Proverb

If you take responsibility for yourself you will develop a hunger to accomplish your dreams.
Les Brown

"Greatness is not measured by what a man accomplishes, but the opposition he or she has overcome to reach his goals.
Dorothy Height

Most important things in the world have been accomplished by people who have kept on trying when there seemed to be no hope at all.
Dale Carnegie

Be the change in the world you want to see.
Mahatma Gandhi

The fifth freedom is freedom from ignorance.
Lyndon B. Johnson

QUOTATIONS

I have to look at my past, but I don't have to stare at it.
Author unknown

We so often look so long and so regretfully upon the close door we do not see the ones that open for us.
Alexander Bell

Faith is believing things will turn out like it should.
John Woods

First say to yourself what you would be and then do what you have to do.
Epictetus

Nurture your mind with great thoughts for you will go to no higher than you think.
Benjamin Disraeli

A wise man should consider that health is the greatest of human blessing, and learn how by his own thought to derive benefit from his illness.
Hippocrates

You must take responsibility. You cannot change the circumstances, seasons, or the wind, but you can change yourself. That is something you have charge of.
Jim Rohn

I believe life is a series of near misses. A lot of what we ascribe to luck is not luck at all. It's seizing the day and accepting responsibility for your future. It's seeing what other people don't see and pursuing the vision.
Howard Schultz

QUOTATIONS

The way you think, the way you behave, the way you eat can influence your life by 30 to 50 years.
Deepak Chopra

I determined never to stop until I had come to the end and achieved my purpose.
David Livingstone

Move out of your comfort zone. You can only grow if you are willing to feel awkward and uncomfortable when you try something new.
Brian Tracey

Success usually comes to those who are too busy to be looking for it.
Henry Thoreau

Motivation is a fire from within. If someone else tries to light that fire under you, chances are it will burn very briefly.
Stephen Covey

Knowledge is power, the more knowledge, expertise, and connections you have the easier it is for you to make a profit at the game of your choice.
Stuart Wilde

More men fail through lack of purpose than lack of talent.
Billy Sunday

The purpose of life is a life of purpose.
Robert Byrne

My business is not to remake myself, but to make the absolute

best of what God made.
                                        Robert Browning

Contact Information:

K. R. Shelton International
P.O. Box 533
Muskegon, MI 49443

Phone: 313.427.1671

Email: krsheltonsr@aol.com

www.kensrspeaks.com

www.achievingsuccessthroughadversity.com

KEN SHELTON

Quick Order Form

Telephone orders: 313.427.1671

Email orders: krsheltonsr@aol.com

Postal Orders: K. R. Shelton, International
P. O. Box 533
Muskegon, MI 49443, USA

Please send the following books or disks to:

Please send more free information on:
_____Speaking Engagements _____Consulting

Name _____
Address _____
City _____
State _____ Zip _____
Phone (day) _____ evening/cell _____
Email _____

Shipping U. S. $5.50 for first book, $4.50 for CD, and $2.50 for each additional product. International $9.00 for first book or disk; $5.00 for each additional product.

Sales tax: Add 7.75% sales tax for products shipped to California addresses.

Payment: ___Visa ___ MasterCard ___Optima ___Amex ___Discover
Card Number: _____
Security code: _____
Name on card: _____
Exp. Date: _____

www.ingramcontent.com/pod-product-compliance
Lightning Source LLC
Chambersburg PA
CBHW060834050426
42453CB00008B/688